LOOKING AFTER
YOUR MAC
MADE EASY

2019 EDITION

Publisher and Creative Director: Nick Wells
Project Editor: Polly Prior
Art Director and Layout Design: Mike Spender
Digital Design and Production: Chris Herbert
Copy Editor: Anna Groves
Technical Reader: Mark Mayne
Proofreader: Amanda Crook
Screenshots: Chris Smith

Special thanks: Laura Bulbeck, Emma Chafer, Esme Chapman, Helen Snaith

FLAME TREE PUBLISHING
6 Melbray Mews
Fulham, London SW6 3NS
United Kingdom

Screenshots courtesy of Chris Smith/Flame Tree Publishing. All Apple product shots, as well as that on page 157, are © **2014/2019
Apple Inc.**; all other non-screenshot pictures are courtesy of **Shutterstock.com**: 38, 219 and © the following photographers: aastock:
7, 212; aksenova_sveta 34; ALPA PROD 172; Andrey Bayda: 4, 14; Beboopai: 230; DAMRONG RATTANAPONG: 166; Goodluz: 132, 189;
Dmitry Lobanov: 77; Krisda: 161; Halay Alex: 226; imagedb.com: 204; Kaspars Grinvalds: 5, 84; Kirill__M : 6, 152; ra2studio: 6, 136;
sdecoret: 5, 42; sheff: 7, 180; Tomislav Stajduhar: 227; tkemot: 222; woottigon 191.

ISBN 978-1-78755-729-1

Manufactured in China

1 3 5 7 9 10 8 6 4 2

LOOKING AFTER YOUR MAC MADE EASY

2019 EDITION

CHRIS SMITH

FLAME TREE
PUBLISHING

CONTENTS

If you're yet to plump for a brand new Mac and you're still weighing up your options, this chapter will furnish you with all the information you need to make sure you come home with the perfect model for your needs. You'll also learn about the advantages of using a Mac over a PC and the best accessories to augment your Mac. Finally, we'll get that new Mac out of the box and introduce and explain some of its physical features, before getting it ready for action.

GETTING STARTED

This chapter will guide you through the initial set-up process and explain the basics of macOS (formerly known and Mac OS X). You'll learn your way around the user interface, how to master the dock, take a trip around the software with Finder, get connected to the Internet, learn the basics of using applications, and master some neat multi-touch gestures for good measure.

PUTTING YOUR MAC TO WORK

Now all of the basics are out of the way, we'll really start to pick up the pace in this chapter. We'll learn the intricacies of the Safari web browser, get productive, get organized, and set-up your email, messaging and social-networking accounts. We'll also give you the low-down on finding and downloading apps, and organizing your photo collection and storing it safely on your Mac.

ENTERTAINMENT

A shorter chapter aimed at helping you get the most out of your digital movie and music collection through iTunes. We'll also introduce the Books store, the App store and the possibilities for gaming on your Mac.

NETWORKING AND SHARING

Now we're getting into the technical stuff. Within these pages, you'll learn how to create the perfect home network, incorporating all of your accessories and home entertainment equipment. We'll also explore other ways to get connected, how to create computer-to-computer networks, and how to share files with other devices.

Here you'll learn to safeguard your precious documents, photographs, media files and applications. You'll learn how to back up your Mac, master the powerful iCloud and Time Machine tools, and we'll also give you all of the information you need to keep your Mac secure from unwanted intrusion.

Are you struggling with a maddeningly slow Mac? Unable to access your files? Enduring terrible battery life? Fret not, we've got the solution. And, if your Mac encounters a serious problem beyond our expertise, we'll point you in the right direction.

INTRODUCTION

If you're reading this book, then congratulations are in order. You've either decided to buy a Mac computer, or you've already taken the leap into a brave new world of computing. Whether this is your first computer, or you're taking a journey into the unknown from the familiarity of a Windows PC, you've come to the right place. By the time you're through with this book, you'll be a Mac master, an expert at setting up and getting the most out of the software, able to protect your important data and squash any problems you may encounter. We're excited and we hope you are too.

Yum.

Think different.

WHAT CAN I DO WITH A MAC?

One of the questions we get asked most often is: 'Can a Mac do everything a PC can?' The answer is a resounding yes, and then some. As you'll discover, it's a productivity-enhancing device for work and school, a comprehensive communications tool for messaging, video chatting and emailing, and it's perfect for getting the most out of the Internet and social networks. It's a multimedia powerhouse, a navigation tool, a personal organizer, and a place to store and share your photos. If you're a creative type, then there are tons of powerful apps you can use to make your vision a reality. What more could you ask?

Left: Macs have the capabilities to do everything PCs can, and may even be more suited to certain purposes, particularly creative projects.

Above: The design of Mac computers is constantly changing and improving, with the latest versions looking particularly sleek and slim.

A QUICK HISTORY LESSON

Mac is short for Macintosh, the line of computers created by American technology giant, Apple. You know, the guys who have since become more famous for the iPod, iTunes, iPad, iPhone and Apple Watch. Apple's history runs deep. It was co-founded by the late Steve Jobs in 1976 and, before the Microsoft monopoly took over, a Macintosh was the first computer in many homes during the revolution of the 1980s. Apple faded as Windows dominated the 1990s, but thanks to stunning design and intuitive software, Apple has bounced back strongly in the 21st century. What's more, if you're one of the millions who own an iPhone or an iPad, you're going to get even more out of your Mac!

WHICH MAC IS BEST FOR ME?

Macs might be in the minority when it comes to the number of Windows PCs on sale, but that doesn't mean there isn't a host of awesome options to choose from. If you've already chosen your Mac, you're all set, but if you're still deliberating, the first part of Chapter One will help you work out which Apple computer is best for you. From the ultra-portable MacBook Air, to a 27-inch desktop iMac. We'll also help you calculate how much processing power, memory and storage you'll need.

THE macOS SOFTWARE

All Apple Mac computers run off built-in software that's made by Apple and Apple only. It's called macOS (formerly known as Mac OS X), meaning the tenth version of the Macintosh Operating System. The current version is macOS 10.14, more commonly known as Mojave. If you're on a Mac bought in the last few years, you can upgrade to Mojave for free. If you're buying a new Mac, it's built right in when you switch on for the first time. We think you'll find it intuitive and easy to use. We'll be talking through the features assuming you're using Mojave. Where features are new in Mojave, we'll make you aware, in case you're on an older version.

Above: Throughout this book we will discuss how to use macOS software, both current and older versions where there are differences.

USING THIS BOOK

While this book has been written with a logical chronology – from buying a Mac, to setting it up, to learning the software and putting it to work – it doesn't mean you need to read it from cover to cover. We hope that you'll dive in whenever you need help or something explained in simple terms. We've also given special consideration to Chapters Six and Seven. They'll help you look after your new computer as well as navigate the myriad issues and problems that can pop up with any complex electronic device.

Easily Digestible

Make no mistake, there's a LOT of information contained within the next 250 or so pages, but there's no need to be intimidated. As far as possible, we've broken it down into bite-sized chunks. In some areas we'll offer a general explanation of features and their capabilities, while in others there'll be detailed step-by-step instructions. We've also illustrated many of the features with screenshots so you can see what you're doing. In order to get the most out of this book, we suggest you're seated in front of your Mac as you read.

Jargon Busting

It's true that some jargon is unavoidable, but wherever possible we've attempted to explain and break down technical terms in easy-to-understand language.

Seven Chapters

While we've chosen to spread the path to becoming a Mac expert across seven clearly defined chapters, we'll nudge you in and out of other chapters when features overlap. Chapter One is all about finding the perfect Mac for you and getting it set up. Chapter Two guides you through the initial set-up and will familiarize you with the basic features of the macOS operating system. In Chapter Three you'll put your Mac to work, and in Chapter Four we'll have a little fun with music and video content. In Chapter Five we'll perfect networking in home and public, while Chapter Six is all about protecting your Mac and the information stored within. In Chapter Seven we'll run through a host of common problems and zap them one by one, and if we can't zap them, we'll point you in the direction of someone who can!

Left: You will be guided through all the basics to get you started, such as setting up an Internet connection.

Above: Chapter Four will discuss everything you need to know about working with music and videos on your Mac.

Apptastic

If you've just spent hundreds of pounds or dollars (and often much more) on a Mac, the last thing you want to do is spend a fortune on expensive programmes. With that in mind, we've focused on the apps that are built in with your Mac, mentioning other freebies here and there. However, at the end of the book you'll find a list of 100 fantastic apps you can download to take your user experience to the next level.

About The Author

Chris Smith is a freelance technology journalist for some of the UK's most respected websites and publications. Chris has been using, testing and reviewing Macs for over ten years and has written countless articles about Apple computers, software and applications during that time.

SETTING UP

WHAT IS A MAC COMPUTER?

Mac computers are made by Apple and Apple only. That's the same company that's responsible for the wildly successful and popular iPhone smartphones, iPad tablets and iPod music players. Before the mobile gadgets took over, Macs were where it all started for Apple. The company launched its first home computer in 1984 and after disappearing into the wilderness during the 1990s, it's remerged with a vengeance over the last twenty years.

WHAT MAKES A MAC DIFFERENT?

Other than the hardware designed and built by Apple, what distinguishes Mac computers from the personal computers you may be used to? Mainly, it's the software. Computers with the Apple logo operate on the macOS (Macintosh Operating System) rather than the Microsoft-build Windows software that most PC users will be used to. macOS software behaves very differently to the Windows operating system, but different can be good and is assuredly so in this instance.

Left: The first Apple Macintosh home computer.

WHICH MAC IS BEST FOR YOU?

There are lots of different Mac models around so it's very important to choose the correct computer to suit your needs. Do you work a lot on the go, or do you need a powerful machine, with a big display for your home office? Here are your options.

Apple iMac

The iMac is Apple's staple desktop computer, and is great for the home office. The newest models are things of real beauty. The iMac comes in an all-in-one package with all of the computing technology housed within a thin, fully adjustable display. The iMac comes in 21-inch or 27-inch models with a 4K display if you wish.

MacBook Pro

The MacBook Pro brings all of the power and functionality of a desktop iMac in one portable, lightweight package that can be carried around with you wherever you go. Naturally, this laptop computer comes with the display, keyboard and trackpad integrated within one neat package and the choice of a high-resolution 13-inch or 15-inch 'Retina' display.

Hot Tip

The Mac Pro is only really for those needing to deal with massive amounts of data at high speed, well beyond what would be required by the vast majority of computer users.

Left: The MacBook Pro with Touch Bar offers a mini touchscreen, allowing for different shortcuts depending on the apps you're using.

MacBook Pro With Touch Bar

A couple of years ago Apple launched a new version of the MacBook Pro with all the power and panache of the original, with a brand new digital Touch Bar. This touch-based strip is in place of the function keys on the keyboard and dynamically changes depending on the app you are using. It also has a Touch ID fingerprint sensor. These models are more expensive.

MacBook Air

The MacBook Air is lighter and thinner than the MacBook Pro, but not as powerful. It is the most affordable Apple laptop of all and has a 13-inch screen. The high-end 2018 model has a Touch ID fingerprint sensor for added security and a high-resolution Retina display, but a base model without either also exists.

Apple MacBook 12-inch

There's an Apple MacBook that's even slimmer and lighter than 'Air'. This one's just called MacBook and has a 12-inch Retina Display. It has 10 hours of battery life, weighs just 2lbs and is 13.1mm thin. These are more expensive than the MacBook Air.

iMac Pro

This machine is the pinnacle of the Apple computing innovation and costs around £4,900/$5,000. Designed only for those creative professionals who seek the ultimate power for video editing, game development and more. It has a 27-inch 5K resolution display (better than most modern televisions).

Mac Pro

The freestanding tower requires a monitor and accessories, but provides phenomenal power and memory capabilities. It costs from £3,000/$4,000.

Mac Mini

Refreshed in 2018, The Mac Mini is a good option for those who already have a monitor, mouse and keyboard. The Mac Mini box, named for its diminutive size, simply connects to your existing accessories.

Above: The Mac Mini is perfect if you already have a lot of computer accessories like a monitor, keyboard and mouse.

Ideal Use Cases

- **MacBook Air and MacBook 12-inch**: Light user, Internet surfer, email addict, traveller, writer, commuter.

- **MacBook Pro**: On-the-go power user, working from home, designer, music editor.

- **MacBook Pro with Touch Bar**: The above + photo/video editor, designer, movie fan.

- **iMac 27-inch**: Slave to the desk, movie fan and design fetishist.

- **iMac Pro and Mac Pro**: Professional HD video editor, web designer, music producer, game developer.

WHERE ARE ALL THE TOUCH SCREEN MACS?

Short answer? There aren't any and there aren't likely to be any anytime soon. Apple has been reluctant to cannibalize Macs and iPads by creating a hybrid model because the company believes there is room in our living rooms (if not our bank balance) for both. If you want a touch screen Mac, the closest you'll get is an Apple iPad and a Bluetooth wireless keyboard. Failing that, it'll be one of the many Windows 10 tablet/laptop hybrids. But before you do that, read on.

MAC VERSUS WINDOWS

The on-going war between Mac and personal computers running Microsoft's Windows operating system continues to rage. Quite frankly, and depending on your sport, it's the technological equivalent of Liverpool and Manchester United, Borg and McEnroe or Muhammad Ali and Joe Frazier.

THE RIVALRY: A POTTED HISTORY

The first versions of the Apple Mac dominated the 1980s and for many households it was their first computer. Apple somewhat lost its way in the 1990s and, largely as a result of the launch of Windows 3.0 in 1990, Microsoft assumed the dominant position it still holds today.

By that time home computers were almost as prevalent as the television set. Apple fought back in the Noughties (or whatever we're calling them) with the launch of the macOS software (a huge upgrade), but Mac ownership still makes up the minority.

Above: Apple launched the Mac OS X software in the Noughties. It is known as macOS.

WHY CHOOSE A MAC?

As most people learn to use a computer using Windows, the change to Mac, which runs very different software and uses a slightly different keyboard, can be somewhat confusing. This book aims to assist you with the transition and to outline some of the benefits you can look forward to when you've made the switch.

Less Viruses

Windows PCs are always going down with some kind of infection or ailment and require expensive anti-virus software to stave off terminal illness. Those threats are far less common on Mac computers, with very few recorded incidents of malicious software affecting users. Apple says 'no computer is 100 per cent safe', but its machines are *safer*.

Great Design

Generally speaking, Macs are infinitely better looking than their Windows-running counterparts. Design is Apple's thing. Heck, the company's British design guru Jonathan Ive was recently awarded a knighthood for it. Arise, Sir Jony!

Hot Tip

To learn about how to protect your Mac online, head on to Chapter Six (*see* pages 180–211).

Above: One of the most appealing things about Mac computers is the beauty of their design.

Space Saving And Portability

The all-in-one iMacs and the newest MacBooks defy modern physics with their ultra-thin and light designs. That's a big plus for modern users who don't want bulky tower PCs cluttering up the home, or to carry cumbersome laptops to work every day.

Intuitive Software

There's a saying among Apple fans: 'Once you go Mac, you never go back!' As soon as you've mastered the intricacies of the macOS software, you'll wonder why you toiled for so long on Windows.

Powerful Tools For Creative Types

If you look at the creative industries – publishing, design, entertainment – all of the top dogs use Macs rather than PCs. If you're designing a magazine, editing video, producing music, Mac is where it's at. If your creative juices are overflowing, you're more likely to channel them using a Mac.

Above: Macs can often be a better choice for those working on creative projects.

Playing Nicely With iPhones And iPads

A lot of people become interested in owning a Mac because they love the user-friendly experience of using an iPad or iPhone. There's more symmetry than ever between Apple's mobile and computing software and, as you'd expect, these devices communicate very well with each other. Email, calendar documents, photos, music, video and more come together in one cosy ecosystem.

Above: iPads are compact and perfect for simple needs such as browsing the Internet and listening to music.

Speaking Of iPads ...

Now because you've bought this book, or are at least reading it at your local library or bookstore, we're pretty sure you're set on buying a Mac. Not that we'd ever try to convince you otherwise, but before you do, answer these questions truthfully:

- Do you enjoy playing lots of games like **Angry Birds**?

- Do you plan to use your **Mac** mainly for looking at the Internet, emailing **friends**, watching **video** and listening to **music**?

- Do you prefer using **touch screen** devices to physical **keyboards**?

- Could you survive without access to full productivity programs like **word processors**, **photo editors** and **design tools**?

- Are you looking for the most **compact** package possible?

If the answer to most or all of these questions is '**Yes**' then you may want to consider buying an iPad. Just sayin'.

> **Hot Tip**
>
> Use iTunes and Photos on your Mac to back up and safeguard the data and photographs on your iPhone (*see* page 120).

WHAT TO LOOK FOR

Once you've decided which Mac model is for you, there are many configuration options to decide upon before completing your purchase. The most important of these are the display size, the amount of computing power (CPU), the memory (RAM) and the amount of built-in storage your device has. All of these can significantly affect the price, so choose wisely.

DISPLAY SIZE

This is kind of an obvious one and often the first and most important choice for users. MacBooks range from 12-inches inches to 15.4 inches. If portability is your key concern, then the 12-inch MacBook is for you. If you're editing photos or watching a lot of movies, then maybe choose the 15.4-inch MacBook Pro. The same goes for the iMacs at 21- and 27-inches. Remember, the larger the screen, the larger the price.

PROCESSING POWER

When purchasing a Mac, either through the Apple Store or your local electronics retailer, they'll ask you about processors (CPU). The better the CPU, the more efficient your computer will be at performing the tasks asked of it. If you're only using your Mac for web browsing, document creation and emailing, you won't need to overspend on CPU, but if you try power-hungry tasks on that machine, you'll see plenty of the annoying spinning beach ball (see page 217). Don't expect to edit high-definition video on a MacBook Air; for that you'll need a MacBook Pro or iMac.

Right: The processing power needed on your Mac computer will depend on the types of tasks likely to be performed.

- **Intel Cores**: The newest Macs run on the latest generation Intel Core i5, i7 or i9 chips. The top-end i9 chips represent higher performance and hence add to the cost of your Mac. The base MacBook model uses a lower-powered Intel Core m3 meaning it is less suited for intense tasks.

- **Dual core, quad core or more**: It's quite simple, the more cores in your processor, the more power it provides. Dual-core (two cores) processors are standard in Macs, but the high-end iMacs offer an Intel i9 processor with a whopping eight cores.

- **Speed**: When choosing your processor you'll see a speed attached to the processor. That's how fast it's capable of running. A 2.3 GHz dual-core Intel Core i5 processor on an iMac won't offer the performance benefits of a 3.0 GHz 6-core Intel Core i5 processor.

MEMORY

A lot of people confuse memory with the amount of stuff you can store on your computer. That's not the case. RAM, which stands for Random Access Memory, is the computer's short-term memory, where all of your current tasks are handled. The more things you're doing on your Mac or the more power-hungry programs you're using, the more memory it takes up. The more memory your computer has to spare, the more efficiently it can accomplish these tasks. The MacBook Airs come with 8 GB of RAM, while the iMac Pro is configurable to 256 GB of RAM. You can do the math there.

Hot Tip

On some MacBook models it's very difficult to add RAM due to the unibody casing. If you're in doubt, it's better to go big on memory when you buy your Mac.

Above: One way to boost storage space is to connect an external hard drive to your Mac.

STORAGE

This is where all of your files sit. If you have a massive personal music and video collection or a huge photo library to store on your Mac, then the 128 GB MacBook Air is going to fill up very quickly. Of course, more storage adds to the cost of your Mac.

GRAPHICS

This isn't a huge concern for newcomers, but if you enjoy gaming on your device, then a better graphics card will be of assistance with the large transfers of visual data. Numerous configurations are available.

ACCESSORIZING

You've navigated the minefield of configuring your Mac, but before you hit the checkout button or hand over your credit card, you may want to accessorize your Mac. Here's some of the stuff you may need/want/can't afford but will buy anyway.

Optical Drive

The era of physical media seems to be coming to an end, in favour of an all-digital future. To that end, Apple has ditched disk drives (for DVDs and CDs) in all models.

Hot Tip

There are multiple ways to boost your storage. You can buy an external hard drive that plugs into your Mac, or use iCloud to store your files.

That means if you want to play your physical movie and music collection, you'll need a Superdrive. They cost £65/$79 and plug into your Mac's USB ports.

Above: A Superdrive.

Mouse Or Trackpad?

When buying an iMac, you'll need to choose whether you want a traditional Apple mouse or a Magic Trackpad. Using the trackpad you'll navigate around the OS using your fingers on the flat surface and tapping to click. It's pretty cool once you're used to it, and when ordering from Apple it comes at no extra cost.

AirPort Time Capsule

We'll go into more detail about this in Chapters Five, Six and Seven, but the AirPort Time Capsule is an external hard drive that also backs up all of your data at regular intervals, wirelessly, saving your skin if something happens to your Mac. It's also a fully functioning wireless modem, too.

Above: A Magic Trackpad can be used to navigate the screen instead of a traditional mouse.

Printer

Thanks to the joys of email we don't kill nearly as many trees as we used to, but printers are still handy occasionally. Macs are compatible with wireless and wired USB printers, so take your pick. If you already have one at home, it should still hook up.

External Hard Drive

If you choose an AirPort Time Capsule you're covered for storage space, otherwise you may want to buy an external hard drive in order to back up your documents and store media collections that have become too large for storage on your Mac. These supplemental storage drives plug in through the USB port or the Thunderbolt port on newer Macs.

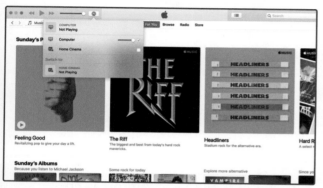

Above: AirPlay can stream music and videos from iTunes.
Below: The Apple TV device sends content from the Mac to the TV.

External Speakers

All new Macs come with built-in speakers, but there's nothing wrong with boosting the sound output a little. Macs will hook up to any speakers with a 3.5-mm (headphone-sized) jack, but you may wish to look at AirPlay and Bluetooth speakers (see page 168) which allow you to beam audio from your Mac over the airwaves without being tethered to wires.

Apple TV

Imagine being able to send content from your computer directly to your HD television over the Internet! Well, it's pretty straightforward actually, thanks to the Apple TV device. As well as being able to send video to the big screen using AirPlay technology (see page 170), you can completely mirror what's on your Mac screen, making it great for showing photo slideshows or even presentations. The Apple TV costs £139/$149.

Need Wired Internet?

Mainly as a space-saving measure, which allows Macs to be more portable, Apple has foregone the Ethernet port on Mac laptops, which means you can only connect to networks wirelessly. It's a bit of a pain sometimes, but if you still want or need to physically tether yourself to a network, you can buy a £25/$29 adapter with your Mac.

Protection

After splashing all this cash on a Mac, it'd be remiss not to give yourself a little protection. Here are a few ways to do this.

- **AppleCare**: When you buy a Mac you're covered by a one year limited warranty which covers you for repair or replacement when the issue is not your fault (drops, liquid damage, etc. aren't covered), but Apple's extended warranty programme covers you for damages after that period. You'll also get telephone support as well as free repairs for three years after the original purchase date.

Above: AppleCare offers extended support after the initial 90 days warranty.

- **Cases**: There is a huge array of cases, bags and clip-on shells to keep your MacBook in pristine condition and safeguard it against occasional drops and spills. Get one. You won't regret it.

Hot Tip

Brenthaven cases and backpacks come highly recommended, while the see-through, clip-on coatings from Speck are also very popular and will keep your Mac looking sharp. Shop around online for some good deals.

GETTING FAMILIAR WITH YOUR MAC

Okay, so you've finally chosen the Mac that best suits your needs and it's sitting there looking all pretty in a box in your living room. Before we jump into the joys of the macOS software, let's take a tour around the hardware and get it set up properly.

UNBOXING YOUR MAC

Regardless of the time of year, there's something extremely Christmassy about unboxing a brand-new piece of tech, especially when it comes in as nice a box as an Apple iMac or MacBook! Let's take a look at what's inside.

What's In The Box?

The packaging is minimal because, unlike big PCs of yesteryear, there's not a lot in the box other than the essentials.

- **MacBook/Air/Pro**: When you open your MacBook, you'll find only the computer itself, the MagSafe power cable, an AC adapter and a little bit of documentation. All of the software is pre-installed, so you're ready to go.

Above: The MacBook Air comes with just a few essentials. The software is already installed.

Above: An iMac will come with a wireless keyboard, as well as a power cable and wireless mouse or trackpad.

- **iMac/iMac Pro:** If you've bought an iMac or iMac Pro you don't have to worry about separate monitors and tower units because it comes in such a tight, all-in-one, space-saving package. In the box you'll have the power cable, along with the wireless mouse/trackpad and wireless keyboard. As with MacBooks, all software is pre-installed on the device.

- **Mac Pro:** Barely anything. You get the unit itself and the power cable. Everything else (keyboard, mouse/ trackpad and monitor) is sold separately.

- **Mac Mini:** The Mac Mini is aimed at those who already have a bunch of equipment, so there's little in the box apart from the power cable.

A QUICK TOUR AROUND THE MAC HARDWARE

Now you've got your Mac out of the box, you'll see a host of buttons and connection ports in various positions around the computer. Figuring out what goes where can be quite tricky at first. Here's a helpful guide to what's on show.

Above: MacBook power buttons are top right of the keyboard. On new MacBook Pro and Air models, it's combined with a Touch ID sensor to authenticate your identity.

Power Button

No prizes for guessing here. This is how you switch your Mac on, but it can also be used to put the computer to sleep and wake it from hibernation. On MacBooks it appears on the top right of the keyboard. On newer iMacs it's hidden away around the back.

Trackpad

All MacBooks have a rectangular box below the keyboard that's slightly indented into the body. Give it a rub; you'll notice it's slightly smoother than the rest of the casing. This is how you'll navigate around your Mac and select objects on screen. You use a finger to move the cursor or press down to click and make your selection.

Hot Tip

The trackpad is smarter than it looks. It offers a series of multi-touch gestures where you can use more than one digit, pinches, swipes and more to perform different actions.

Trackpad

Ports

Your Mac computer is not an island. To get the most of it, at various times, you'll be plugging in other devices, headphones, power cables, external hard drives, memory cards and so on. In recent years, Apple is placing less and less ports in favour or portability. In many cases it means you need adapters to use accessories.

- **USB-C/Thunderbolt**: The latest generation MacBooks have one or more USB-C ports. These multi-purpose ports allow you to charge your laptop, insert accessories that enable connections to an external monitor, an additional hard-drive, or to charge other devices using the power from your laptop's battery.

- **USB 3.0**: The standard USB ports we're used to are only available on iMac, Mac Mini and Mac Pro laptops. This enables a much wider range of accessories to be added without the need for an adapter.

- **Charging port**: Now this one's pretty essential. MacBook battery life is getting better, but you'll still need to plug in every now and again and iMacs can't run off a battery. On older MacBooks the MagSafe adapter magnetically connects, which means if you tripped over the cable (as we often did) it would just pop out without dragging your Mac down with it. Now MacBooks are charged via USB-C. iMacs and the Mac Mini have a more substantial power cables that are around the back.

- **Headphones**: There's a 3.5-mm jack on all Macs, where you can plug in your headphones, earphones and portable speakers.

- **Memory Card, HDMI and Ethernet ports**: While previously common features on MacBooks

Above: Ports visible on the left side of a MacBook.

they only exist on iMac, Mac mini and Mac Pro these days. They enable you to connect to a HDMI monitor, add a memory card from a camera and enjoy a wired connection to the Internet.

- **Adapters:** Because Apple has cut back on ports, Mac users have relied on a number of adapters (or dongles) to

Above: Ports visible on the left side of a 2018 MacBook Air.

connect a number of accessories. Apple sells a number of options on its website. From a USB-C to traditional USB dongle, which will allow you to plug in a phone, to a Memory Card to the Ethernet cable mentioned above.

PREPARING YOUR MAC FOR ACTION

We've unboxed your new computer. Now it's ready to be plugged in and prepared for take off.

MacBook

New MacBooks come with enough battery charge to get you started, but you'll want to charge it up ASAP. Pop that charging cable into the slot and (sorry to be obvious) plug the other end into the wall. The light on the connector should turn orange to let you know it's charging. It'll turn green when fully charged. Lift the lid on your laptop and you're pretty much good to go.

Above: The Mac Mini.

iMac

iMacs don't have a portable power source and can only run off the mains. Before switching it on, you'll have to hook up the power cable, which plugs directly into the back of the iMac. Don't worry about the mouse and keyboard. We'll get to that on page 44 in the next chapter.

Mac Pro And Mac Mini

Things are a little different for these machines because of the reliance on other, unbundled accessories. You'll need to hook up the power cable *and* a monitor before you can get started. Most modern monitors will be plugged into the HDMI socket (*see* above). If you're using an existing, wired keyboard and mouse, then plug them into the USB sockets. Wireless peripherals can be set up on start up.

GETTING TO KNOW THE MAC KEYBOARD

There are a few subtle differences that separate the Mac keyboard from the standard keyboard PC users will be used to, but it's easy enough to adjust. Whether it's the keyboard attached to a MacBook or the wireless version that arrives with new iMacs, you'll be shortcutting your way around the keyboard in no time.

① Command key: This is the most important key on the Mac keyboard. Often known as the 'Apple' key, it performs many of the functions of the control key on a PC keyboard, in that it can be combined with others to perform common functions. Command + Q quits a program, Command + S saves a document, while Command + X, C, or V represents cut, copy or paste.

Power button: As referenced earlier in this section, on MacBooks the power button sits in the top right corner of the keyboard.

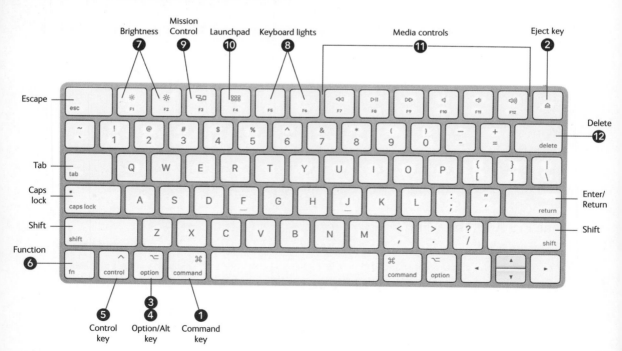

Hot Tip

To close all open windows in Finder (*see* page 62), hit Option + Command + W.

2 **Eject key:** For iMac, Mac Pro or Mac Mini keyboards, where the device is switched on with a button on the device itself, the button in the top right corner of the keyboard allows for discs to be ejected.

3 **Option key:** A useful yet under-utilized key, this is often combined with oter keys, such as Alt, Command and Shift, to perform specific tasks.

4 **Alt keys:** Alt shares a key with Option (they're pretty good friends), and is great for accessing symbols on the keyboard. It's especially good when typing words from foreign languages (Alt + E, then E = é).

Hot Tip

For a full list of Mac keyboard shortcuts – of which there are too many to mention here – check out Apple's official list at http://support.apple.com /kb/ht1343

5 **Control (ctrl) key:** A lesser-used key, but one that comes in handy very occasionally for less essential functions. It's particularly useful in text-editing programs. For example, Control + E moves the cursor to the end of the line.

Hot Tip

Brightness doesn't affect colour temperature of the screen. To reduce harmful 'blue' light, enable Night Shift. The display colour will ease to an orange or yellow as the evening draws on. Head to System Preferences > Displays > Night Shift.

6 **Function (fn) key:** Useless on its own (like Control, Shift, Alt and Option, incidentally), the Function key is used in conjunction with the F-keys on the top row to perform specific actions. They're pre-programmed (for example fn + F9 shows the dashboard) but these features can be customized in System Preferences.

7 **Brightness:** The two keys next to the escape button increase and decrease screen brightness.

8 **Keyboard lights (MacBooks only):** Speaking of working in the dark, the keyboard backlight keys (F5 and F6) can be used to alter the illumination of the keyboard.

9 **Mission Control:** We'll discuss this feature in more detail in Chapter Two, but hitting the icon next to the F3 key activates Mission Control, showing users all open application windows. This feature also sits in the dock.

10 **Launchpad:** Another useful key (F4), this takes you to a screen showing all available apps. This feature is called Launchpad and also sits in the dock.

11 **Media controls:** When playing music or watching video, these keys can be used to play/pause, scan back and forth as well as mute, increase or decrease volume.

12 **Delete:** This one is only slightly confusing. The delete key is effectively backspace when typing. Holding the Function key (fn) will delete words or items in the other direction.

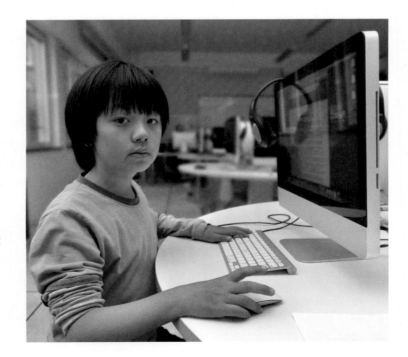

Escape, Caps, Tab, Shift, Enter/Return: In the case of these computing staples, they act in exactly the same way as they do on a PC.

WHAT'S ON THE INSIDE?

Your brand-new Mac is teaming with cutting-edge tech. We've discussed some of it already in the What To Look For section (CPU, RAM, graphics, etc.), but here are some of the other goodies inside your Mac that make the magic happen.

Wi-Fi

Well, you didn't think it connected to the worldwide web by magic, did you? The Wi-Fi chip inside your Mac accepts wireless Internet signals from compatible models, meaning you don't have to plug in to use the Internet.

Bluetooth

Bluetooth is a wireless transfer technology that allows information to be sent over short distances. It's great if you want to chat on a wireless headset, send sound to compatible speakers, or transfer files between other computers and gadgets.

Above: The Wi-Fi and Bluetooth icons sit next to each other on the menu bar.

Microphone

You can barely see this little blighter on most Macs. It lives on the left side of MacBooks and just above the Apple logo on new iMacs. It's tiny but important for any voice-related activity. When chatting on Skype or FaceTime (see page 104) the microphone automatically kicks in so your voice can be heard.

Speakers

It's always good to have a decent pair of speakers for playing your music and movie collection. However, before you go out and buy expensive speakers, you should know your Mac has them built in too. They're especially good on the new desktop iMacs.

Webcam

MacBooks and iMac computers all have the iSight webcam built into the display. You can see it right above the screen. The webcam is capable of snapping stills photos, recording video and transmitting video over the Internet.

Webcam

Hot Tip

For longer-lasting battery life, only keep open the apps you're using, and keep the screen brightness at a reasonable level.

Battery (MacBooks Only)

One of the main reasons to plump for a laptop rather than a desktop computer is the ability to use it on the go, perhaps in the park or the back garden, on planes and trains, in coffee shops and libraries, or even on the sofa when you're not close enough to the wall socket. That's made possible by the ever-improving battery cells of MacBooks.

Software

We haven't talked much about software yet. All of that fun stuff will come in the next chapter, but just so you know, the latest version of the Macintosh operating system (at the time of writing, that's macOS Mojave) is built into your new Mac. If for some reason it's not, then it's a free upgrade, but we'll get to all that stuff. Just know that your Mac is ready to use out of the box.

On that note, let's get started....

Above: macOS Mojave is the latest version of the operating system.

GETTING STARTED

POWERING UP AND SETTING UP

Before you get into the nitty gritty of learning to use macOS, you'll need to go through the initial set-up. Everything is extremely straightforward, but this section will guide you through what to click and what not to click.

POWERING UP

Push that button, we know you've been dying to. Almost instantly you'll hear the trademark Apple chime and an Apple logo will appear, backed by a black (it's grey on older models) screen. In about 30 seconds time you'll be able to get going. New Macs run macOS Mojave, this is how to set it up.

Above: After pressing the Power button, this screen will appear.

Pairing Up The Peripherals (Desktop Macs Only)

Desktop Mac users need to pair up their wireless peripherals before progressing further in the set-up process. Thankfully, with brand-new iMacs the keyboard and trackpad recognise each other from the happy time they spent together at the Mac factory.

1. When you first power on your Mac press the power button on your mouse/

trackpad and keyboard. A green light will indicate they are powered on. The accessories will pair up immediately.

2. When the set-up screen pops-up, move the cursor around using the mouse or trackpad. This will indicate it is working. We'll come to the keyboard in a second...

Choosing Your Region And Keyboard Layout

This is your Mac's way of asking: 'Where you at?' Firstly, you need to select your location from the list of countries in the drop-down menu, then hit Continue. The next screen asks you to select the keyboard language. Make sure you choose English US or UK, depending on your preferences, as there are some subtle differences.

Connecting To Your Network

Next, your new Mac will ask you to select a Wi-Fi network. If you have an Internet connection at home, then this shouldn't be too stressful. Select your network ID from the list of in-range connections (it'll be printed on a sticker on your broadband modem), then type in the password (also printed on the sticker) on your newly connected keyboard and hit Continue.

Above: Select the correct country from the drop-down menu.

Wired Network (Ethernet)

If you wish to use a wired connection, plug in an Ethernet cable (using an iMac/Mac mini/Mac Pro or an adapter for MacBook) and select the Other Network Options button on the Wi-Fi screen. Then select Local Network (Ethernet) from the options and follow the on-screen instructions. See the chapter on Networking (pages 152–181) for more detailed information.

Migration Assistant

If you have information on another Mac or Windows PC you can transfer it to this Mac. You can also transfer information from a Time Machine backup or other startup disk.

How do you want to transfer your information?

○ From a Mac, Time Machine backup, or startup disk
○ From a Windows PC
○ To another Mac

Quit   Continue

Above: It is easy to transfer files from another or computer or disc on to your Mac.

Hot Tip

At any point in the set-up you can hit the Back arrow to alter any information. Likewise, nothing you input during set-up is set in stone. It can all be amended later.

Transferring Your Data?

In recent versions of the macOS software, users are able to transfer all of their files over from other computers they have. This is great if you're a Windows user transferring over to Mac for the first time.

The options are From Another Mac, From A Windows PC or From Another Disc. We'll discuss this in more detail later, as it's something that can be done at a later date using the Migration Assistant. For our purposes, hit Not Now and continue.

Location Services

Your Mac contains a GPS chip that can determine your approximate location. This comes in handy when performing Internet searches for something like movie screening times, restaurants in your vicinity, or directions using a service like Apple Maps. To allow Location Services, click the tick box and press Continue.

Entering Your Apple ID

Do you own an iPhone, iPad or iPod touch? Then you will most likely have an Apple ID account. It can be used on Macs to setup the iTunes Store, the Mac App Store and the iCloud back-up service. If you have one, but don't want to set it up yet, you can skip this step.

1. If you have an Apple ID, enter the email and password associated with the account and hit Continue.

2. If you wish to use a different Apple ID for iCloud and iTunes, then hit that option to configure settings.

3. You can also recover your password or ID, if you've forgotten either or both using this screen.

Above: If you already have an Apple ID, simply enter your email address and password.

The Paperwork

Next, you'll need to accept some of those pesky terms and conditions. There's no way around it. Hardly anyone ever reads these, but you can click the various services (iCloud, Game Center, iTunes, etc.) to see exactly what you're agreeing to, or just blindly accept by hitting the tick box and then Agree.

Connecting With The iCloud

If you've entered your Apple ID (*see* page 47), you'll have the opportunity to configure your Mac with iCloud. This means you'll be able to sync things like email, documents, Internet bookmarks, notes and contacts.

Siri

Apple brought the Siri personal assistant to macOS a couple of years back. It enables you to use voice commands to access functionality, play music, open apps, search the web and more. You can skip this, turn it on now and even enable 'Hey Siri', which enables you to use the assistant without pressing a button first.

Above: Enable iCloud in order to sync various applications.

Getting The iMessage Out

The next screen allows you to configure the accounts at which users can reach you through the Messages chat app and the FaceTime video chat service. Macs running newer versions of OS X can send and receive free SMS messages from others using an Apple device, either through the Mac, iPhone, iPod touch or iPad. All of those messages sync back to all devices, thanks to iCloud.

If you've agreed to iCloud, all of the email accounts/phone numbers already associated with that Apple ID will appear and you can tick/untick those you'd like to use. Once you're happy, click Continue.

Keeping Tabs On Your Mac

Don't worry, just a few more screens to go. Here you'll need to decide whether you'd

Hot Tip

You can use Find My Mac to lock or wipe all of your computer's contents remotely, preventing your sensitive data or photos getting into the wrong hands.

like to use iCloud to track your Mac's location. Should your computer be mislaid or stolen, you can log into iCloud.com and use the Find My Mac service to track its location. It'll even play a sound if you've mislaid it in your home!

Above: Setting up your Mac correctly at the beginning will get you up and running without delay.

Creating Your Computer Account

Even if you don't feel like using Find Your Mac, you definitely need to create a password for your computer to keep potential intruders out. On this screen you input your name, choose a name for your computer's Home file and, most importantly, add a password. Try to choose something that's easy for you to remember, but something no one else will guess. Don't use your name or date of birth!

Pick Your Pic

The account screen also allows you to customize your Mac with a profile picture. By clicking the square box next to the name, the Photo Booth camera interface will load and you can take what the kids refer to as a 'selfie' using the webcam. This can be changed with a fancier pic at a later time.

Hot Tip

Make sure the 'Require password when logging in' checkbox is ticked. The password will also be used to change settings, install software and administer your computer, so make it a good one.

Adding The Magic Touch

The MacBook Pro with TouchBar and the 2018 MacBook Air have a Touch ID fingerprint sensor that uses your fingerprint to unlock your Mac, authorise payments and more. It's more secure than a password, so if you have it, use it. It involves you

Above: Load the Photo Booth interface and take a photo of yourself to use as your profile picture.

registering your fingerprint multiple times and following the set-up instructions on screen. You can add an additional print later at System Preferences > Touch ID on compatible Macs.

Light Side Or Dark Side?

New in macOS Mojave is the option to choose a dark mode theme, which uses various shades of black and grey rather than the standard white. Some users find this easier on the eyes, especially at night. As with everything here, this choice isn't permanent. You can amend this in System Preferences > General later.

To Register Or Not To Register?

On this screen Apple asks you for your postal and email addresses in order to get faster access to support. This isn't entirely necessary, so you can skip for now if you wish.

Step Up Is Complete!

Woo and indeed hoo! The next screen congratulates you on navigating the set-up minefield. Do yourself a favour: click that button that says 'Start using your Mac'. Welcome to your brand-new Apple Mac. Let's get started.

A CLOSER LOOK AT macOS

Once set-up is complete you'll be taken straight to your Mac's desktop. Every function on your Mac computer can be accessed from this point in some way, shape or form.

WHAT IS macOS?

As we alluded to in the previous chapter, the software you now see before your eyes is called macOS. It's made by Apple for Apple computers. Simple as that. If you're using a brand-new Mac it is extremely likely that you're using version 10.14, which is known as Mojave.

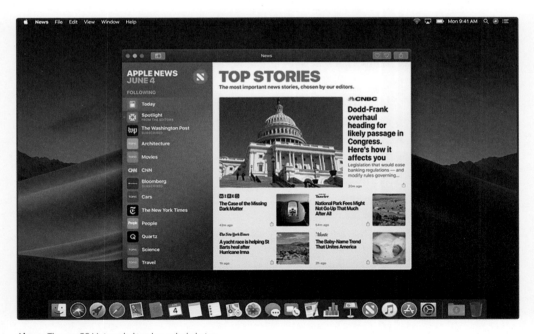

Above: The macOS Mojave desktop has a sleek design.

Which Version Of macOS Are You Using?

Apple introduced Mac OS X (the tenth version of its computing operating system) as a pre-loaded feature of all Macs in 2002 and it's been a staple ever since. It's now known as macOS. Every year it gets a fresh lick of paint with some new features that's free to download and install. Here's a brief guide to the last few releases:

- **macOS 10.14 Mojave (2018)**: The main feature addition was the new dark mode, the Stacks file grouping tool, access to iOS (iPhone and iPad) apps, Group FaceTime calls, a redesigned Mac App Store and improved screenshot tools.

- **macOS 10.13 High Sierra (2017)**: A new Apple Files system, a massively improved Photos app, a faster Safari web browser and smoother video.

- **macOS 10.12 Sierra (2016)**: The first to use the new macOS naming convention, Sierra integrated the Siri voice assistant, Apple Pay on the web, a revamped Messages app and the ability to unlock a Mac with an Apple Watch.

- **Mac OS X 10.11 El Capitan (2015)**: El Capitan included a revamped Spotlight search tool, the ability to view two apps in split screen and improvements to many of the core apps we still use on Macs today.

- **Mac OS X 10.10 Yosemite (2014)**: Here Apple improved interoperability with iPhones and iPad devices, enabling users to hand-off tasks like emails to the mobile devices and exchange files easily via AirDrop. It also added the iCloud Drive online document storage platform.

Upgrading To Mojave

If you're using a slightly older Mac and want the latest and greatest software features, then you can upgrade to macOS Mojave free of charge. It's available to Macs running OS X 10.8 Mountain Lion and above. You can see compatible models here: http://support.apple.com/macos/mojave. If you're good to go, let's get you bang up to date.

Above: If your Mac is compatible with macOS Mojave, it doesn't cost anything to upgrade it.

1. Make sure your data is backed up first. While software updates don't often cause problems, it's better to be safe than sorry (*see* page 182).
2. Open the Mac App Store and search for 'Mojave' or click 'Updates'. Once you've found the page, click the 'Get' button to begin downloading the operating system.
3. It may take a while to download the operating system update, but once complete simply go through the install process and follow the on-screen steps.
4. You'll be running macOS Mojave in no time at all.

Hot Tip
If you're not sure which version of macOS your computer is running, hit the Apple logo in the menu bar and select About This Mac.

Above: About This Mac offers key system information.

macOS BASICS

We're guessing you've had enough of the history lesson and set-up stuff by now. In front of you is a blank desktop canvas waiting to be filled and a dock full of apps waiting to be put to use. Without further ado, let's do some exploring.

Above: Click the Finder icon on the dock to bring up a Finder window, and access your files.

THE BIG FOUR

Once start-up is complete, you'll see the macOS desktop. At this stage it's probably easier to split the general user interface into four sections. There's the desktop, which dominates most of the Mac's display, the dock at the bottom of the screen and the menu bar at the top of the screen. There's also the Finder functionality, which is the closest thing to the Windows start button you'll see on a Mac. Before we go into detail, let's introduce all four.

The Desktop

Right now the majority of the display is covered only with the macOS wallpaper, but pretty soon you'll be

Hot Tip

To see all open app windows on the screen, hit the Mission Control button on your keyboard (F3). Move the cursor to the app of your choice and click.

loading up the desktop with files, folders, photos, software and more. Naturally, when any apps are open they appear within this space, layered on top of each other depending on which you're using.

Above: Press F3 on the keyboard to bring up Mission Control. This shows you all open apps.

Finder

Finder is a very important part of the macOS experience. As the name suggests, the Finder window offers fast access to everything on your computer. Opening a Finder window offers fast access to every file, folder, application and programme. When you're working on the desktop, you're already in Finder mode, while clicking the Finder icon in the dock brings up a window.

Above: The Finder function offers a fast way to access your applications and files.

Hot Tip

When working on the desktop hit Control + N to open a new Finder window.

Above: Save your most commonly used programs to the dock for quick access to them.

The Dock

The macOS dock is awesome and a signature of the user interface. It's a home for all of your favourite programs and represents a simple way to open and switch between all of your software. If an app is open, its icon sits neatly in the dock. Go ahead, move your cursor over one of the application icons and click it; it won't bite!

Above: The menu bar hosts both features for the currently open app and general information.

The Menu Bar

The translucent bar at the very top of the screen features commands for the app you're currently using. For example, for Mail you'll see the name of the program next to the Apple logo, followed by File, Edit, View and all that good stuff. However, there's also a host of static icons at the right edge of the screen, which inform you about battery life, Internet status, the time and more. Tap these menu items for more options.

NAVIGATION BASICS

Here are a few basic skills you'll need to master, along with some tips to help you master the keyboard, mouse and trackpad.

USING THE MOUSE OR TRACKPAD

Without a mouse or trackpad it's nigh on impossible to do anything with your new Mac. Go on, try it and see how far you get. Moving the mouse with your hand or moving around the trackpad by lightly pressing down and dragging a finger, moves the cursor in the desired direction.

Clicking And Right Clicking

Whether you're using a traditional mouse, a Magic Trackpad or a laptop trackpad, you can push down to click and select the option your cursor is hovering over. The act of 'right clicking' traditionally accesses options within specific apps (if you right click an app in the dock, you can quit it), but you'll notice there's no 'right' button on the Mac mouse or trackpad as there is on a Windows PC. To get around this you can a) click the trackpad with two fingers rather than one or b) hold the Control button as you click the mouse or trackpad.

Above: One method of right-clicking on an icon is to hold the Control button as you click the trackpad or mouse.

Above: To delete a file, use the drag and drop method to select the file and move it into the Trash.

Dragging And Dropping

If you want to move items around your Mac, dragging and dropping is an important tool. For example, if you pick up a song file, drag it and drop it on to the iTunes icon within the dock, and that song will open in iTunes and begin playing. If you drag a file on to the trash bucket within the dock and drop it, it will be placed in the Trash.

To drag and drop, click on a file and hold down the mouse or trackpad button. With the button still held down, move the mouse or use a different finger to move the trackpad to the new destination and release the mouse and trackpad. Simple.

Keyboard Shortcuts

You can perform a lot of popular tasks on your Mac by performing simple keyboard shortcuts. A keyboard shortcut is achieved by hitting a combination of two or more keys at the same time. We'll mention many of these as we go along, but here are some of the simplest and most commonly used. Remember they perform differently within different apps.

Command + A = Select all items within a window

Command + B = Make selected text bold in documents

Command + C = Copy all selected items to the clipboard

Command + D = Add a bookmark when using Internet browsers

Command + E = Eject a CD or DVD (if an optical drive is present)

Command + F = Access the search box within a given app (F = find!)

Command + I = Get information about a file or folder/Make selected
text italic in documents

Command + M = Minimize a window

Command + N = New document, new file, new window, new playlist, etc.

Command + O = Open a file

Command + P = Print

Command + Q = Quit a program

Command + R = Refresh a webpage

Command + S = Save

Command + T = Open a new tab in Finder
or in the web browser

Command + U = Underline selected text
within documents

Command + V = Paste selected items

Command + W = Close the current window

Command + X = Cut selected items

Command + Z = Undo the last action

Some of the more complex actions require more than two keys. For example:

Command + Option + Esc = Force Quit app menu

Command + Option + M = Minimize all windows within an app

Command + Shift + 3 = Take a screenshot

Command + Shift + 4 = Draw a custom screenshot

USING THE DOCK

As we mentioned previously, the dock is one of your best friends on the Mac. From set-up it is jam-packed across the board with Apple's stock applications. Here you'll find things like Finder, Mail, the Safari web browser, iTunes and the App Store.

Above: The Dock is split into segments, with your chosen apps, open/select apps and others like minimised apps, folders and the trash can.

Opening Apps In The Dock

This is the easy part. Move the cursor down to a particular icon in the dock such as the compass, which represents the Safari web browser. As you hover over the icon you'll see the icon will magnify slightly and the app's name appear in a speech bubble. Simply click the icon with your mouse or trackpad.

If the app is already open, it'll bring that window to the forefront of the display. If the app is closed, the icon will begin to bounce and open the app in at the point it was last closed.

Customizing The Dock

As you get to know your Mac you'll want to make the dock more efficient. That means ditching the programs you don't use and adding the ones you use a lot. You can also change the size, visibility and position of the dock. Here's how.

1. To keep an open app in the dock at all times, right click the icon within the dock and select Options, then Keep in Dock.

2. To remove an app from the dock, right click the icon, select Options and untick Keep in Dock. Alternatively, grab the app icon, drag it out of the dock and release. It'll disappear in a puff of smoke.

3. You can also hide the dock from constant view so it only appears when you move the cursor to the very bottom of the screen. This can be handy to ensure it doesn't interfere with other apps. Head to System Preferences, select Dock and then tick Automatically hide and show the Dock.

Step 5: Alter the size of the icon when magnified by sliding between Min and Max.

4. To alter the size of the dock, enter System Preferences, select Dock and pull the scroll bar left or right to make it smaller or larger.

5. To alter the scale of the magnification when the cursor hovers over apps, enter System Preferences > Dock and drag the scroll bar towards Min or Max. You can even untick the box to turn magnification off.

6. If you don't like the dock at the bottom of the screen you can move it to the left or right by selecting a Position on screen button within the dock preferences.

The Dynamic Dock

The macOS dock is smarter than before. It's divided into two sections featuring the apps you've stored there and other apps you may have open. If you've been using an app regularly, that unopened app icon may also sit within the dock because Apple is anticipating you'll use it.

Step 6: The dock does not have to run along the bottom of the screen; it can be moved to the side.

WORKING WITH FINDER

Finder is an essential navigation tool when looking for files, apps and folders within your Mac. Think of it as your command centre. Here's how to master it.

Opening The Finder Window

There are a couple of ways to access and open a Finder window on your Mac. The easiest is to head to the dock and click the first icon, which looks like two smiley blue faces. That'll immediately open an existing Finder window, or begin a new one. If you're working on the desktop, Finder is the default app that appears in the menu bar. You can either hit Command + N to open a new window or File > New Finder Window.

Above: The Finder window has a sidebar with access to favourite items.

Touring The Finder Window

Okay, there's plenty to see here so let's take things slowly and talk through each of the relevant sections, starting with the Favourites sidebar. Hitting one of the options within the sidebar will populate the adjacent section. From here you can use the mouse and trackpad to scan and select files.

- ○ **Recents:** The default view in Finder is the Recents section, which shows every single folder on your computer, starting with the most recent. This is handy if you're looking for recently accessed or downloaded files.

- ○ **AirDrop:** More on this in Chapter Five, but simply put AirDrop allows you to send and receive files from other close-by Macs and Apple devices.

- **Desktop**: Shows a list of all files saved to your desktop.

- **Documents**: Everything you have saved within your Mac's Docments folder.

- **Downloads**: This is helpful when you've obtained files from online sources. Unless you've specified otherwise, they'll be saved in this folder.

- **Movies and Music**: These two options give access to your media files.

Hot Tip

To control what appears in the Favourites sidebar, hit Finder in the menu bar followed by Preferences and Sidebar to tick/untick items.

- **Applications**: You'll probably use this one a lot. It's a shortcut to a list of applications you have installed on your Mac.

- **Pictures**: Your photo library and other pictures are saved to this default folder.

- **Home**: The home folder is usually named after your computer's account and also features a progressive path to items on your computer.

Above: Select Desktop from the sidebar to populate the adjacent section with files saved there.

Quick Look

Quick Look, the eye icon within the Finder window toolbar, is a very useful feature. Selecting a file (or multiple files) and hitting Quick Look will immediately show a preview of each file, without the need to open the full app. This is very useful if you need a closer look than the thumbnail. From here you can share the file via Mail, Messages and others, or open it in another app.

Above: Quick Look allows you to preview a file without opening the app.

Back And Forth

As you progress through the file and folder paths in Finder, sometimes you'll need to backtrack to the previous screen. This is enabled by the useful arrows in the Finder window.

Above: The column view in Finder can make it easier to browse between folders.

Changing The View In Finder

The window also boasts a view section allowing users to choose how the files appear. Hitting these icons allows you to view thumbnails (useful for photographs), files in a long list (useful when looking for documents), files in column view (opening up the file path) and as Cover Flow, which shows thumbnails that can easily be whizzed through.

Deleting Files Using Finder

The view offered within the Finder window makes it easy to delete unwanted files your Mac. If, for example, you're looking through the Downloads folder, you can select those you wish to delete and then hit the trashcan icon in the Finder window. This will move those files to the Trash, which you'll see within the dock.

Selecting Multiple Files

Sometimes you'll want to open/share more than one file at a time. Instead of clicking all of those files individually, you can batch them together and perform the task in one fell swoop. Here's how.

1. To select more than one file: Click the file of your choice, then hold down the Shift key and click the last item in the list you wish to select. This will group them all together and highlight them in blue.

2. To pick and choose the items you wish to select, pick one file and hold down the Command key and click each one individually.

3. From here you can right click on one of the files, or hit the Action icon in the Finder window and choose the group action. Perhaps it's Open, Open With (a particular app), Share or creating a new folder.

Step 3: Once the files are selected, right click and select the action you want to perform to all.

Moving Files Around In Finder

To prevent your Mac becoming a big unorganized mess of files and programs, you'll need to do a bit of organizing here and there, grouping things together in specially created folders or moving items from one folder to another.

1. To create a new folder within a Finder window use the shortcut Command + Shift + N. It'll appear under the name 'untitled folder'. You can just start typing and then hit enter to give it a name.

2. To move items into the folder, select the files in question (see page 65) and drag and drop them into the newly created folder.

Hot Tip

To move easily between tabs, use the keyboard shortcut Command + Tab.

Above: Finder windows can have multiple tabs, so no need for several Finder windows.

3. You can also drag and drop selected files into Trash, on to/an application icon within the dock to open them in that app, or move them to any of the Favourites folders listed in the sidebar, for example, the Documents folder.

Finder Tabs

One of the more helpful Finder features is tabs, which means you don't have to have multiple Finder windows all over the place. To open a Finder tab use the keyboard shortcut Command + T. Additional tabs can be opened using the '+' icon in the top right corner of the window.

Searching Using Finder

Well it wouldn't be a very good Finder if it didn't allow you to search, right? Thankfully, within the window there's a box dedicated to finding what you need by name. Move your cursor into the box and start typing. This will immediately show files, folders and apps with matching names on your Mac. Also listed is the folder within which you began the search. Hit this to narrow down the results.

Sharing Using Finder

The Finder also represents an easy way for you to share files and folders with others. Once a file is selected within a window, you can hit the Share icon in the toolbar, which presents available options. For example, photos can be shared via Mail (opens a new email message complete with the attached file), Messages (likewise) or through Airdrop, Notes and More.

Above: Select a file and then click the Share icon at the top of the Finder window.

Customizing The Finder Window

Like most things on a Mac, the Finder window itself can be customized to look exactly how you wish, adding or subtracting items for personal preference. For example, if you right click on the toolbar you'll see the Customize Toolbar option appear.

Selecting this option presents a menu packed full of icons that can be dragged and dropped (see page 58) directly on to the toolbar. Say, for example, Get Info, which you can press in order to learn more about a selected file, it can be pinned to the toolbar.

WORKING WITH THE MENU BAR

The menu bar sits across the top of the display at all times and offers application-specific commands as well as a host of information about the key functions of your Mac. Hitting each of the items in the menu bar opens a drop-down menu, allowing you to select relevant actions.

Above: The Apple logo provides access to key functions on your Mac.

Apple Logo

One thing that's always there is the Apple logo in the top left corner. Beneath this button, you'll have a shortcut to a few of your Mac's key functions. You can open the System Preferences app to modify your settings, access the App Store and Software Updates, open recent documents and, if the work or play is done for the day, you can choose to put your computer to sleep, restart it or shut it down completely.

It's All In The Name

If you have lots of windows open, it's easy to lose track of which app you're currently controlling. This is solved by a quick look to the top left of the menu bar. For example, as I type this document, my Mac says 'Word'. From this menu, you can access the app-specific preferences and quit the program.

Other Headers In The Menu Bar

As we mentioned above, the other headers vary depending on the app you're working with at the time. Here are some of the most common.

○ **File:** Here you can create new items, open existing items, save, share, print and more.

- **Edit**: Another common header in most apps in macOS. Here you'll be able to cut, copy and paste selected items, as well as access the undo last step and redo features.

- **View**: View generally controls the appearance of the application; what you see and what you don't. For example, in the Safari web browser, you can View > Show/Hide Sidebar.

Above: The Edit menu allows you to copy and paste amongst other functions.

- **Window**: This function can be used to minimize or maximize particular windows or to choose which window to bring to the front of the screen.

- **Help**: Help is ever present. Here you can type in questions and you'll mostly be presented with easy-to-understand answers.

HOW THE OTHER HALF (of the Menu Bar) LIVES

While the left side offers access to app-specific tools, the icons to the right are always present, irrespective of which app you're in. They show connectivity status, remaining battery life, the time and much more. Here they are, from right to left.

Above: Icons on the right hand side of the menu are not specific to whichever app is open, but give more general information.

Stay Notified

We'll talk more about Notifications in the next chapter, but the list-like icon you'll see within the menu bar is how you access them. Opening this reveals a sidebar on your Mac showing recent emails, messages, forthcoming calendar appointments and social-networking tools. From here you can also control which notifications you receive and how they appear on screen.

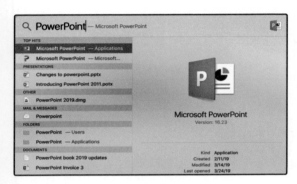

Above: Press Command + Space or hit the magnifying glass icon in the Menu bar to search your Mac.

Siri

Some MacBook Pro laptops have a dedicated Siri button in the Touch Bar, but for everyone else, there's an option in the menu bar. Click it to bring up the assistant. It will sound a tone, which means it is ready for your voice commands.

Putting Your Files In The Spotlight

Spotlight has been an integral part of macOS since its inception and is the easiest way to find absolutely anything on your Mac, whether it's an app or a file or even a key word within emails, messages or documents. Just hit the magnifying glass and start typing and results will immediately begin populating below.

[Your Name Goes Here]

Most of the time, your name will sit next to the Spotlight magnifying glass. This is to let you know which account is in use. Macs can have multiple user accounts for both security and convenience. Clicking the name allows users to switch between accounts from the drop-down menu.

Keeping Track Of Time

Do you ever get so absorbed in creating that office PowerPoint presentation that you lose all track of time and space? No, us neither, but having a clock there sure does help sometimes. Clicking the clock will also show you the date.

Battery Life

iMac, Mac Mini and Mac Pro users can skip this bit, but for MacBook users this is probably the most crucial part of the menu bar. When the battery is off charge you'll see a percentage of how much is left. When it gets into the red, you've got less than 10 per cent left and you'll need to plug in. When plugged in, the reading will still show the remaining battery life.

Volume Rocker

There are a couple of ways you can adjust the system volume on your trusty Mac. One is with the on-keyboard buttons (F10/F11/F12), the other is with the slider in the menu bar. Hit this and drag the volume up and down. There's a visual representation of the current volume at all times.

Above: Click this icon to check the Internet connectivity status of the Mac.

Are You Online?

This icon is pretty crucial too as it shows your Internet connectivity status. If the signal bar is full, it means you're online and have great signal. The bars will drop if you're connected to a network, but have a weaker signal. If you're offline, the bars meter will be empty, while if you're unable to connect to a network an exclamation point will appear in the meter. If Wi-Fi is turned off, you'll see a hollow meter. If you click the Internet meter, you can choose to join a different network from the drop-down menu, turn Wi-Fi on and off (this is sometimes helpful if you briefly lose connectivity), and also access Network Preferences.

Other Menu Bar Items

You can put anything you want to in the menu bar. Apps like Skype also make their presence known when in use. You'll also see icons for modifying AirPlay, Time Machine and Bluetooth settings. There'll be more on these throughout the book.

Hot Tip

Your Mac has a great memory and remembers every place where you've connected to a Wi-Fi network. Next time you visit that place you'll automatically be connected to that network.

WORKING WITH YOUR DESKTOP

The desktop is useful as a place to store files and folders that don't necessarily have an immediate home, such as email attachments, new documents and anything that you'd like to have at hand without delving through the file paths.

Organizing Your Desktop

The desktop can get quite messy from time to time, but there are plenty of ways to bring some order to the chaos, by arranging the icons. Right click on an available area of the desktop and hit Clean Up By or Sort By to arrange the icons by Name, Date, Size, Last Opened or More.

Above: Right click on the desktop and select Clean Up By in order to organise the files on the desktop.

Above: macOS Mojave has a neat new Stacks feature that will keep your desktop clean without any additional work.

Stacks

macOS Mojave introduced an automatic way to tidy your desktop, called Stacks. It will group together likeminded items like pictures and screenshots. It should be enabled by default but you can turn it on or off by selecting Finder and choosing View > Use Stacks from the Menu bar. Here you can also choose how the stacks are grouped.

Hot Tip
To access your desktop at any time without minimizing or closing your app windows set up a Hot Corner (see page 75).

Changing The Desktop Background

The default wallpaper that ships with macOS is lovely and all, but we'd prefer a picture of our mother's dog. To change the desktop background, right click on a free part of the desktop and choose – you guessed it – Change Desktop Background. Here you can select from the default options or use one of your own photos.

Above: Personalize the desktop background with your picture of choice.

View Options

You can also customize the size of the file icons, and whether text and information is shown alongside them by right clicking and hitting Show View Options and playing with the settings.

Saving To Desktop

Whenever you're saving a file, be it an email attachment, a Word document or a photo, you'll often be asked where you'd like to save it. If you'd like to dump it on the desktop for convenience, just use the Command + D keyboard shortcut when within the Save dialogue box.

Above: To save an item to the desktop, press Command + D within the Save dialogue box.

MULTI-TOUCH GESTURES AND HOT CORNERS

These two pieces of macOS functionality are part of what makes using Macs so enjoyable. With a simple swipe or pinch on the trackpad or by moving the cursor into one of the four corners you can perform actions more easily than ever.

Getting Used To Multi-touch

Inspired by the touch screen gestures on the iPhone and iPad, multi-touch gestures on Mac computers add functionality to the trackpad, using two or more fingers to perform certain actions. Apple offers a neat description and animations of available gestures at System Preferences > Trackpad, but here are some of our most used gestures.

- **Two fingers in any direction**: Scroll around individual windows and documents. The movement follows your fingers and means you don't have to use in-app scroll bars.

- **Swipe left or right with three fingers**: Move between full-screen apps or access the dashboard (*see* page 119).

- **Pinch with two fingers**: Zoom in or out on photos and other items.

- **Swipe down with three fingers**: Access App Exposé, which shows all open windows within an app, allowing you to easily move between them.

- **Swipe up with three fingers**: Access Mission Control, showing all open apps left or right with two fingers: move between pages in a window. Can be a handy alternative to the back/forward arrows.

- **Spread thumb and three fingers**: This will show the desktop and allow you to interact with files saved there.

Above: Trackpad preferences offers descriptions of available gestures.

○ **Double tap with two fingers**: Smart zoom in and out on a page.

○ **Rotate with two fingers**: Rotate an image within an app.

Note: Gestures can be customized and are slightly different when using a Magic Mouse rather than a trackpad.

Mastering Hot Corners

Hot Corners are a great way of getting around your Mac quickly, just by moving the cursor into one of the four corners of the display. You can customize them in whichever way you see fit.

1. Go to System Preferences > Mission Control > Hot Corners. You'll see a new window with four pull-down menus, one for each corner.

2. Select from any of the 9 actions for each Hot Corner. Your options are:
   - ○ Access **Mission Control** (*see* page 78)
   - ○ Show open **Application Windows**
   - ○ Show **Desktop**
   - ○ Show **Dashboard**
   - ○ Show **Notification Center**
   - ○ Show **Launchpad**
   - ○ **Start Screen Saver**
   - ○ **Disable Screen Saver**
   - ○ **Put Display to Sleep**

3. To return to the previous stage, just revisit the same corner. We find Desktop and Application Windows by far the most useful Hot Corners, but it'll vary for each user.

Right: Select Application Windows for one of your Hot Corner actions and you will be able to see all current open applications.

Using The Touch Bar

As we mentioned in Chapter 1, some new MacBook Pro models offer a dynamic Touch Bar above the keyboard. Effectively, it's a mini touchscreen that offers shortcuts to features and common functionality within apps. We won't dwell too much on this because the MacBook Pro with Touch Bar is generally a model preferred by experienced Mac users. Here are some examples of what might be shown on the Touch Bar. You can learn more here: https://support.apple.com/en-us/HT207055

- **Control Strip**: This appears when you turn the Mac on, it offer access to brightness, volume controls and Siri. Hitting the expand arrow will reveal a wider range of controls offering access to Mission Control, Launchpad, and media controls.

- **Share**: When using the Share command the Touch Bar will popular with potential locations like Messages, Mail, AirDrop and more.

- **Safari**: If browsing the web in Safari, you'll see common controls and shortcuts to your Favorites.

- **Mail**: Touch Bar within the Mail app offers word predictions to save you typing, quick access to an emoji keyboard as well as text formatting tools.

- **Calendar**: The Touch Bar makes it easy to tab between months, customize locations, times and invitees.

Above: The Touch Bar on a MacBook Pro will dynamically show quick access to features depending on the app used.

APPLICATION BASICS

You're now familiar with the most essential user-interface tools in your Mac's arsenal, but it's difficult to work or play unless you're familiar with how to use the computer's suite of applications. In this section, we'll show you how to find, open and close your apps.

FINDING AND OPENING APPS

There are a number of ways to browse your Mac's applications, some of which we've already discussed within this chapter.

1. The easiest way is to navigate to them within the dock (see page 60). Click an app to open.

2. Use the Finder > Applications sidebar to see a list of everything that's installed. Double click to open one.

Hot Tip

To place an Applications folder shortcut in the dock, head to Finder > Applications sidebar > right click and Add to Dock. Click the shortcut and select the icon of your choosing to open.

Launchpad

Launchpad, as the name would suggest, is an area of your Mac where every app sits. Hit the space rocket icon in the dock, press F4 on the keyboard or move the cursor into a configured Hot Corner and you'll see a new screen that looks a little like the iPad's layout with a grid of apps. Simply hit the app of your choice to open.

Above: From the Launchpad screen you will see a grid of apps. You can then easily select the app you want.

Moving Between Open Apps

There are a few fun ways to switch apps while keeping others running in the background. The easiest way is to hit the open app icon within the dock. However, there are plenty of other ways to go about it.

Mission Control: Represented by the icon with multiple open windows within the dock and also accessible through the F3 key on the keyboard. It shows a representation of all open apps on your screen. Click on one to move to it.

Above: Hold down Command and Shift, then tap Tab. Keep holding Command and Shift, then select an icon from the menu of open apps.

Command + Shift + Tab: This is a neat little trick. Hold down the Command and Shift keys together and tap Tab. This brings up an on-screen menu of open apps. Continue holding down Command and Shift and pick your app.

Selecting Items Within Apps

To select a block of text on a webpage, in a URL bar, in a text document or within an email, you first need to highlight it. There are several ways to do this.

Hot Tip

Create a Hot Corner (*see page 75*) for Mission Control for even easier access to your open apps.

1. Double clicking a word highlights it, a triple click highlights the entire paragraph or line.

2. Command + A selects everything within the window.

3. Holding down on the mouse or trackpad and using it to move over the area you wish to select, allows you to highlight that area.

Above: To highlight a selection of text on a webpage, hold down and drag the trackpad or mouse over the area.

Once the section is highlighted, Command + C copies the text, Command + X cuts it and Command + V pastes it within an email, document or app. Right clicking serves up a wider array of options, such as the dictionary or formatting options.

MOVING, MINIMIZING, MAXIMIZING, RESIZING

There's plenty you can do to customize your in-app experience.

Minimizing Apps And Windows

To hide a window from view, you can hit the Command + M keyboard shortcut. You'll see a neat genie-in-a-bottle effect as the window descends into the dock. Alternatively, you can hit the amber circle in the top left corner of the window. You can summon it once again by finding it in the dock.

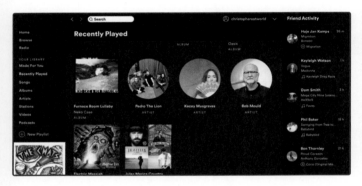

Above: Making apps full screen allows you to focus solely on the current task.

Full Screen Apps

To extend a window so it dominates the entire screen on your Mac hit the green circle in the top left corner of the window. This will launch a full screen apps. You can use three fingers on the trackpad to swipe between full screen apps, or clock the green circle again to return to normal view.

Resizing Windows

You can easily customize how your app windows appear on screen, by placing the cursor in the bottom right corner, holding down the mouse or trackpad and dragging to the new size.

Moving Windows

You can easily move the Windows around the display (or to a different display) by dragging the title bar around the screen.

Going Split Screen

macOS now has a near split screen feature, which enables you to work within two apps at the same time, which is handy if only have a small laptop screen. In order you launch this feature hold down the green circle in the top left corner and release the app on the shaded blue area. You'll then need to click another open app and the two windows will snap together.

Closing Windows

To get rid of a tab or an individual window within an app, there's a simple keyboard shortcut – Command + W. In some apps, if there are unsaved changes you'll be asked to save before it closes. You can also hit the red circle within the window itself to close the window.

Quitting Apps

Having apps open when you're not using them not only adds to the clutter on your screen, but it also drains system memory, slowing your computer's performance and, if you're using a MacBook, adds to battery drain. Here's how to shut them down.

1. Hold down the Command key and hit Q to shut down the app in question. If you're working on a project, you'll be asked to save your progress before you quit.

Hot Tip

When apps are in full-screen mode, you can move between them by swiping three fingers across the trackpad left and right. For more multi-touch gestures, *see* page 74.

Hot Tip

Command + Option + Control + Media Eject (power button on MacBooks) forces all programs to quit, while giving you the opportunity to save progress in each.

Force Quit Applications

If an app doesn't respond for a while, select its name and click Force Quit.

- Preview
- Safari
- TextEdit
- Finder

You can open this window by pressing Command-Option-Escape.

Force Quit

Above: Press Command + Alt + Escape to Force Quit programs.

2. Hit the application name in the menu bar and select Quit.

3. Right click on the app in the dock and hit Quit.

4. You can Force Quit applications (great if they're not responding to you through conventional means) by hitting Command + Alt + Escape. Then you can close apps individually. Beware, unsaved progress will be lost if using Force Quit (*see* image on page 81).

Resuming Apps

Apple macOS has a great Resume feature, which allows you to pick up where you left off in some apps. For example, if you quit Text Edit, Pages or Safari without closing individual windows, those windows and tabs will appear again when you re-open the app.

WHEN YOU'RE NOT USING YOUR MAC

As much as we love using our Mac, it's wise to take a break every now and again. Here are your options when you're ready to pack up for the day, or need to restart your computer.

Sleep Mode

While it's wise to give your Mac a complete break by shutting down or giving it a 'power cycle' every now and again, you can mostly get away with putting your Mac to sleep. This is an extremely low-power mode that preserves all of the apps you're working on without putting strain on the battery or using as much electricity.

1. If you're a MacBook owner simply close the lid to put your device to sleep.
2. Select the Apple logo in the menu bar and hit Sleep.

To wake your Mac from its snooze, you can simply open the lid on a MacBook, hit any key on the keyboard or tap the power button once again. You'll need to log back in using your computer's password.

Restarting Your Mac

There are plenty of occasions where it makes sense to restart your Mac. It can be necessary to complete program installations, it can offer a quick fix for many ills, and it's also good to start with a clean slate every once in a while. Once the restart is complete, log back into your computer and you're good to go again.

1. The easiest way is to hit the Apple logo and scroll down to restart. You'll be asked to save progress in apps as each one closes.

2. To force the instant restart of the computer, hit the Command + Control + power button.

3. Alternatively, hit Control + power button to show the Restart/Sleep/Shut Down dialogue box.

Above: Hit Control + power button to show the Restart/Sleep/Shut Down options.

Shutting Down

Other than a pint of your local's finest ale, there's no better way to underscore a working day than shutting down your Mac for the day. The methods are very similar to Sleep and Restart.

1. Hit the Apple logo and select Shut Down. You'll be asked to confirm with a dialogue box and will be able to save progress in open apps.

2. To force shutdown, just hold down the power button, although this will mean you'll lose unsaved progress in apps.

Hot Tip

A subset of sleep mode is called Power Nap. When enabled, the Mac will periodically check for new emails and iCloud updates too. Enable it in System Preferences > Energy Saver.

Project Manager

Dashboard | **My Projects** | Timesheets | People | Resources

Marketing campaign	44%	Week 12
		M T W T F M
▾ **Research & planning**	**100%**	
Internal brainstorm	100%	Oliver
Client survey	100%	Jesse
Creative brief	100%	
Kick-off	100%	
▾ **Website**	**64%**	
Design	100%	
Slicing, HTML and CSS	100%	
Coding	80%	
Content	40%	
Testing	0%	
▾ **Social media**	**33%**	
Content preparation	50%	
Visuals and images	50%	
Publishing schedule	0%	
▾ **Outdoors**	**17%**	
Design	25%	
Printing	0%	
Guerilla preparation	25%	
▾ **Press and media**	**8%**	
Partner contracts	25%	
Design	0%	
Publishing schedule	0%	

PUTTING YOUR MAC TO WORK

PUTTING THE APPS IN MAC

Your new computer comes with a host of built-in applications, made by Apple, to enhance your experience. Chapter Two dealt in general terms with apps and how to move between them. Now let's take a look at some of the specifics regarding getting the best from these apps.

WHAT HAVE YOU GOT?

Apple would like us all to think, in one way, shape or form, that it offers all the tools you need to achieve all you need on a Mac. While that's not quite the case, the macOS software is a very good start. There's an email app for sending and receiving correspondence, a web browser for

Above: The macOS software may not have everything but it does have a large number of useful apps.

looking at the Internet, a couple of notepads, a photo locker, a video editor, a messaging portal, a media player, a calendar, an address book, a Maps app and many more little widgets.

What Haven't You Got?

So what do you need to buy? Well, there's no Microsoft Office built-in for a start. That means no Word, no PowerPoint, no Excel and no Outlook, but you can get it. There's no Adobe Photoshop either, there's no Skype, no Google Chrome and no Spotify music player. That's the bad news....

Above: Visit the Mac App store to download apps which did not come with your Mac.

How Do I Get Them?

But now the good news. You can get all of those apps, very, very easily, from the Mac App Store, through the Internet or through other portals. A lot of the ones we mentioned are free, while you'll have to fork out a bit of cash for others.

GOING ON SAFARI

Getting online is a primary concern with any computer. Your Mac comes with Apple's own Safari web browser and is represented by the compass icon in the dock. Open it up and let's explore.

Hot Tip

Are you connected to the Internet yet? If not, go to System Preferences > Network for help connecting to your home and public network, or see Chapter Five for full details.

The Safari Window

The default opening page in Safari is really quite useful. It shows thumbnails of the websites you visit most often for easy, one-click access, a list of any pages you have bookmarked for future reference and of course the URL bar where you type in your www dots.

Hot Tip

The Top Sites homepage can be accessed at any time by opening a new tab or by adding the grid option by right clicking and dragging the grid icon into the toolbar.

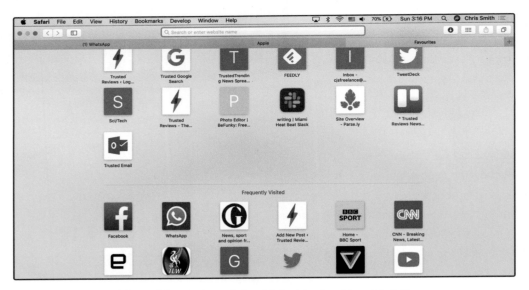

Above: Whenever you start Safari, it will show thumbnails of often-visited websites, for quick access to them.

Opening A Webpage

With the Safari window open, the world (wide web) is your oyster. To open a favourite webpage, let's say bbc.co.uk, place your cursor in the URL bar at the top of the page and click. Then simply type bbc.co.uk on the keyboard and hit the Enter/Return key. A few seconds later (depending on the speed of your Internet connection), you'll see something resembling this....

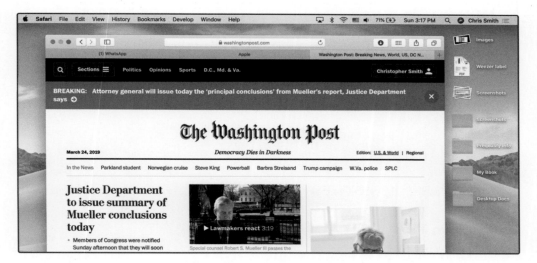

Above: Type in the name of the website, hit enter and simply wait for it to load. It should only take a few seconds.

Searching The Web

The web holds a wealth of information and Safari, via a search engine of your choosing, will help you find exactly what you need. You can browse to your favourite search engine by going to Google.com, Bing.com or whatever. However, you can simply type your search terms into the URL bar. For example, 'restaurants in London' will load applicable results. To set your default search engine, head to Safari in the menu bar and select Preferences.

Start Your Own Tab(s)

You'll want to keep some pages open while you navigate around the web. This is where tabs come in really handy. They allow you to open multiple pages within the same window and easily switch between them, allowing you to keep Facebook, Twitter and Sky Sports open while you listen to the news on the BBC iPlayer or watch a movie on Netflix.

1. To open a new tab in Safari, simply use the keyboard shortcut Command + T or hit the + icon in the top right corner.

Above: Tabs are a handy way to switch between different webpages without having multiple windows open.

2. To close an unwanted tab hit Command + W, or hover over the tab and click the x icon.

3. To move between tabs use Control + Tab or just click the individual tabs. Got it? Good.

Using iCloud Tabs

Are you an iPhone or iPad user running iOS 7 and up? The new Safari brings iCloud tabs into play. This means if you've recently accessed a page on another device associated with your Apple ID, it'll remember that page across your devices, syncing almost instantly via iCloud (*see* page 48).

Hot Tip

The Show All Tabs icon in the top right corner is a neat tool, allowing users to scroll through all open tabs, rather than clicking individual tabs.

This is great if you've started reading an article on your iPhone but want to see it on the larger screen when you get home, or vice versa.

1. On your Mac, click the 'show tab overview' button in the top right corner of the Siri toolbar to see the open windows on your iOS device.

2. To ensure it's working, go to System Preferences > iCloud and make sure you're signed in and that Safari is ticked.

Reading List

Reading List is perfect if you're at work and spot something you might like to read on your lunch break. To add a webpage to your Reading List, simply hit the plus (+) icon within the URL bar. Then, to access the Reading List, click the Show Sidebar icon (looks like an open book) in the Favorites bar.

Safari Basics

Without going into too much detail, here are a few Safari essentials to help you along the way.

Above: Save webpages to your Reading List for quick access later on. To add a page, click the plus (+) icon next to the URL bar.

❶ Back/Forward arrows: Move between pages in a specific tab.

❷ Share icon: Share the link to a webpage via Mail, Messages, AirDrop, Notes, Reminders and more. You can also add it to your Bookmarks or Reading List.

❸ Add favourites: Hit Command+D to add your favourite sites to the bookmarks menu. The bookmarks bar no longer appears beneath the URL bar in macOS Mojave, but you can add it by selecting View > Show Favourites Bar while in Safari.

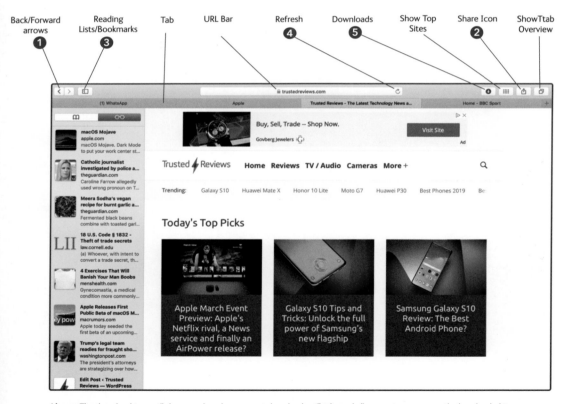

Above: The download icon will show you how long current downloads will take and allow you to open recently downloaded items.

④ **Refresh**: If you want to see the latest version of a webpage (especially if you're following a sports game!) click the curved arrow in the URL bar or use the Command + R keyboard shortcut.

⑤ **Downloads**: Whenever you download a file from the web, be it an email attachment, photo, video or program, you'll see it pop into the download icon in the top right corner. Click this to see recently downloaded files. They can be opened directly from here.

Windows: We've talked about tabs, which we find the best way to work, but if you prefer to work in brand new windows, just use the Command + N shortcut or select File > New Window.

Other Web Browsers

Although Safari is a great browser that comes built into your Mac, it's not the only horse (or zebra?) in the race. Actually, as of recently, it's only taking up about 16 per cent of the market on Mac and PC. Here are some other options.

Above: Google Chrome is particularly good for users of multiple Google services.

○ **Google Chrome:** The world's most popular web browser is available to download at Chrome.com. It's great if you use a lot of Google apps and services like Gmail, YouTube, Google Drive and Google Docs as it synchronizes your experience under one login.

○ **Firefox:** Made by Mozilla, this is another popular alternative which is good for plentiful add-ons, widgets and customization.

SPREADING THE MESSAGE

Another absolutely essential function of any computer is the ability to communicate with friends, family and colleagues electronically. The Mail, Messages and FaceTime apps are built-in solutions but there are plenty of other ways to stay in touch using your Mac.

THE MAIL APP

Thanks to email you can send written correspondence, pictures, videos, documents and practically anything else you desire in seconds. Naturally, your Mac has you covered. The most efficient way to manage your email on your Mac is through the built-in Mail app. It's extremely easy to set up, supports multiple accounts, multiple email providers and it also plays nicely with other applications like Safari, Messages, Photos and iTunes.

Setting Up Your Email Account

You'll find the Mail app within the dock as it's one of the default apps built into your Mac. It's not difficult to find; it's a stamp. Makes sense, right? Click it and once the icon finishes bouncing, you can start setting up your account.

1. You'll see a Welcome to Mail window, which can be by-passed with a click of the Continue button.

2. Choose your account. If you use a webmail service like Gmail, Exchange Yahoo Mail, or AOL, simply select yours from the list. If you use Microsoft Outlook (previously known as Hotmail) or another provider pick 'Add another account'.

3. On the next screen, enter your full name (this will be what the recipient sees when your email arrives) and then enter the username and password that you use to log into

your email account on the web and select Create. If Apple recognizes the account, you should be good to go and emails will begin flooding in.

4. Having trouble configuring your email? Check out page 244.

THE MAIL WINDOW

The Mail app works off a tabbed interface that makes it easy to move between the following tabs (see image on page 96).

- **Mailboxes**: Here you'll see all of your associated email accounts as well as sent messages, drafts, junk, trash and other folders.

- **Messages**: This is a list of the messages you've received in chronological order. Within each box you'll see the name of the sender, the time sent, the amount of messages within the conversation, whether there are attachments, whether you have read or replied to the email and a preview of the email's content. Apple packs a little into a small space here.

- **Conversation View**: The far right tab displays the most currently selected email, along with the content and the conversation as a whole. You can also view any attachments within this window.

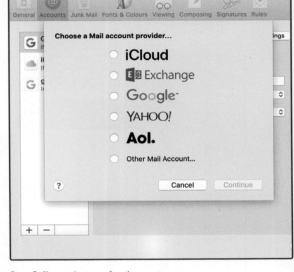

Step 2: Choose the type of mail account you use.

Hot Tip
To add multiple accounts, head to Mail > Preferences in the menu bar. Browse to accounts and hit the + icon. Repeat the process listed above.

- **Toolbar**: There's also a toolbar with access to regularly used commands like New Message, Reply, Reply All, Forward and Delete, while you can also search your mailboxes for content by clicking in the search box and typing names, subjects, content and more.

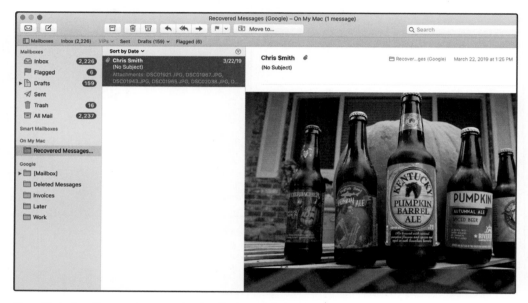

Above: The toolbar offers common commands such as New Message, Reply or Delete, as well as a search box.

Email Basics

Email is all about giving and receiving. To send a brand-new email, hit the pencil and notepad New Message icon in the top left of the Mail window to open a new blank message.

- **To**: Here you'll need to type the email address of your recipient. It'll usually take the form of something like

Hot Tip

If you're having a little trouble getting used to what all of the icons represent within an app, right click on the icon and select Icon and Text. It'll tell you exactly what function a click will perform.

john.johnson@email.com. Regardless of the preface, the @ sign followed by the domain name (@gmail.com, etc.) is essential.

- If you have your contacts set up either through iCloud, or the Address Book app, you can click the blue + and select from your contacts.

- In some cases, if contacts are familiar to the app or the Mac, addresses will auto fill as you begin to type the address or their actual name. This will become more effective the more you use the app, as it remembers addresses you've sent to and received from before.

- **CC**: If you wish to 'copy in' another person, place their email address here. This is usually deployed when an email contains information pertinent to a person, but isn't directly addressed to them.

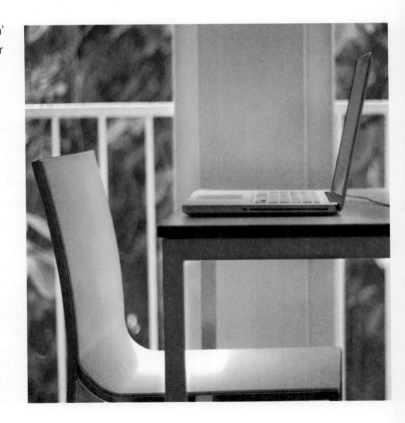

- **Subject**: Just a general description of what the email regards will suffice here.

- **From**: If you have more than one account set up, you'll need to choose which account it is sent from by selecting from the drop-down box here.

Composing Emails

Now that's all of the boring stuff out of the way, you can focus on the content itself, the messages of love, the holiday plans, the funny photographs or the work presentation you're really proud of. Just tap in the empty text box and begin typing. If you're simply sending a text-based email, you can just hit Send and away it goes.

Above: Click the paperclip icon to add attachments to emails.

Adding Attachments

A lot of the time you'll want to add more than just text to your emails. In this case you need to click the paperclip icon in the New Message window. This loads a dialogue box where you can choose which files are to be attached. It looks just like the Finder window, so navigate to your files as you normally would and click Choose File.

Adding Photographs

You can choose a photo by using the adding attachment methods above. However, there's also a dedicated button for adding photos. Clicking this gives you the option to launch the photo browser. However, the best feature is called Continuity Camera and it's new in Mojave/iOS 12 for iPhone. It enables you to take a photo or even scan a document from a connected iPhone.

- Select Photos from a compose email window
- Choose Take Photo
- The camera interface will open on your iPhone
- Take the photo. You can choose to retake or use it. If you pick use it will appear the compose window on your Mac like magic.

Hot Tip

To start a new email with an attachment, simply drag the file name, or icon on to the Mail app. Alternatively, right click a file, browse to Share and select Mail.

Changing The Look And Feel Of Your Emails

In the New Message window you'll see an 'A'. Tapping this opens the text formatting, allowing you to customize fonts, text size, colour, style (bold, italic, underline) and more. Like other apps such as Word, Pages, TextEdit, etc. text must be highlighted before changes are effected. Remember, Command + A selects all text. In the toolbar you'll also see a smiling face. This enables you to include the emojis you know and love from your smartphone within the email.

Receiving Emails

If you've set up your email address correctly (see page 94), emails should come through as they arrive. This is called 'Push' email. It means you don't have to keep tapping the Get Mail button in the Mail toolbar. When a new message arrives, you'll hear an alert and get a notification in the top right corner. Click this to go straight to the email. If you miss the notification, the amount of unread emails you've received appears as a number upon the Mail app in the dock. Pretty useful, if you ask us.

Hot Tip

An unread email in a conversation thread is represented by a blue dot within the Message tab, next to the sender, subject, date and content preview.

Reading Emails

Such is the way the Mail app is configured, you need to do very little to read your emails. Simply choose the Mailbox, select the message from the message list tab and the content will appear in the right-hand tab. If it is part of a conversation, you'll be able to scroll through all of the other emails sent and received.

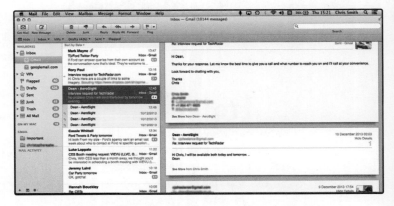

Above: The Mail app allows easy scrolling through messages in the same conversation.

Replying And Forwarding

Within the conversation view on the far right, you have all of the tools you'll need to reply to correspondence. Each of these commands opens the reply in a new window. All you need to do is add your content, further recipients and click send.

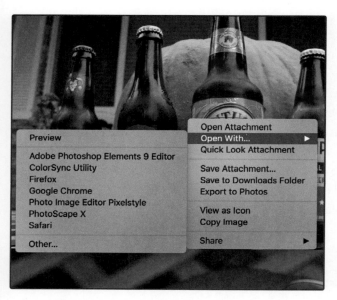

Above: Choose which app you would prefer to open the attachment with, by selecting Open With... from the options.

Opening And Saving Attachments

Attachments will happily sit in your inbox for ever, but you'll often need to act upon them. Right clicking the attachment allows you to do the following.

- **Open:** Opens the app with a default program. For example, photos will always open in Preview.

- **Open With:** Choose the app with which to open. Perhaps you'd rather use Photos?

- **Save Attachment:** Choose where you'd like to keep it on your Mac (Desktop, Pictures, Downloads, etc.).

- **Quick Look:** Quickly reveals the contents of the attachment without the need to fully open in an app.

Hot Tip

You can reply to or delete emails directly from the notification alert that appears in the top right corner when an email arrives.

Deleting Emails

Heaven knows, we all get blighted with email spam and junk from time to time, but it can be dispatched immediately. When an email is selected in the Message view, simply hit Delete, or click the trashcan in the toolbar or the conversation view.

MESSAGES

The Messages app is now a staple of macOS and comes over from the mobile world. It allows you to exchange short messages, photos, files and more with anyone using a Mac and also an Apple iPhone, iPad and iPod touch. It is built into your Mac and is represented by a blue speech bubble in the dock.

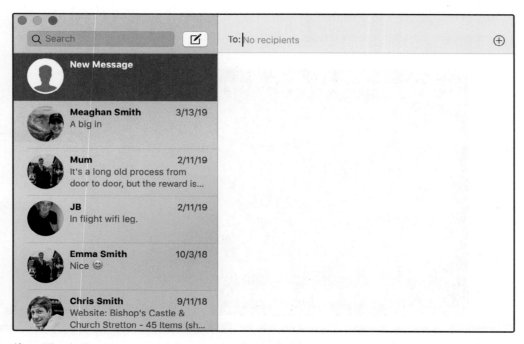

Above: When the Messages app is opened, the message log will automatically appear.

Setting Up Messages

Establishing Messages will be different for different users. Depending on the version of macOS you're using you may be asked to set up messages during set-up. Otherwise open the Messages app, hit Preferences and click iMessage to sign in with your Apple ID. If you're already using an iPhone, iPad or iPod touch for Messages then your account will sync and your message log should start to populate the window.

Sending Messages

As we mentioned, you can send free messages from your Mac to anyone with an Apple ID. That means you can text people's phones using their actual phone number providing they have

Above: Your messages will appear in a different coloured speech bubble to the person you are talking to.

an iPhone and receive replies on your Mac or any other Apple devices you have. Everything is nicely synced through iCloud.

1. To start a new message, hit the pencil and notepad icon in the sidebar and add the iPhone number or Apple ID-associated email address of the person you wish to contact. If your contacts are synced, you can hit the blue + button to find recipients.

2. Then simply type in the text box at the foot of the window and hit enter when you're done. The message will appear above in the conversation view and will be marked with 'Delivered' once it has successfully arrived with the recipient.

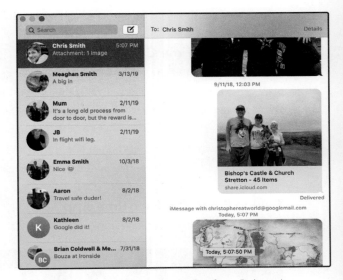

Above: Add pictures to a message by dragging them from a Finder window.

3. All future messages between the two parties will appear within this feed as they appear as text messages on smartphones.

Syncing Your Text Messages

As well as sending and receiving iMessages using your Apple ID, you can also have your text messages synced from your iPhone directly to the Messages app. These will come through even if the other person is using an Android phone. To enable this feature select Messages > Preferences > iMessage and tick the box that says 'you can be reached at' with your phone number next to it.

Hot Tip

In Messages > Preferences > iMessage you can link the app to iCloud so actions you take on your Mac (such as deleting message threads) are reflected in other devices associated with your Apple ID.

GETTING IN A LITTLE FACETIME

Within the Messages app, you can also make free video and audio calls using the FaceTime app. You can make these calls to other Mac, iPhone, iPod touch or iPad users. You'll also find a separate FaceTime app within your Applications folder that enables wider group calls.

Making FaceTime Calls

If you choose to start a FaceTime call from a conversation in Messages (click the name and select FaceTime audio or video), it will summon the standalone FaceTime application, activate the Mac's built-in FaceTime camera (MacBooks and iMacs only) and begin dialling the recipient. Until you get an answer you'll see your own appearance in the window. If the call is answered, you'll sink into the bottom left corner and the recipient will appear. You'll be able to see each other and chat providing your audio is up and your microphone is activated (*see* page 40).

Calling From The FaceTime App

FaceTime has its own standalone app in the Applications folder. Starting a FaceTime

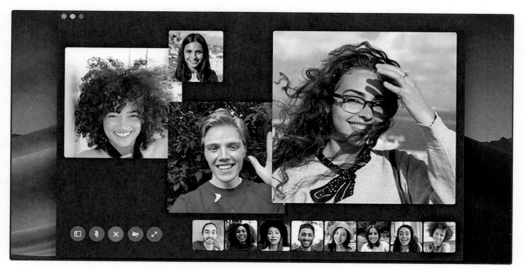

Above: The FaceTime app allows you to make free video calls with other Apple users.

conversation is pretty straightforward if you have your Address Book set up (*see* page 114). From the sidebar search for a contact. Select the contact and then select one of the green Audio or Video buttons to commence the call.

Group FaceTime

macOS Mojave lets you make a FaceTime call with up to 32 people. Just select more than one contact from the search bar. If they're all using compatible devices you'll be able to select the same green audio and video buttons to commence a larger call.

Receiving FaceTime Calls

Naturally, you can also receive incoming FaceTime calls. An incoming call will be greeted with an onscreen graphic, the name of the caller and the opportunity to accept or decline.

Receiving Phone Calls

Just like it's possible to receive your texts in the Messages app, the FaceTime app will also deliver calls from your iPhone too, if you so desire. Select FaceTime > Preferences and tick Calls From Phone. Here you can also select a ringtone too. Your iPhone needs to be nearby and connected to Wi-Fi.

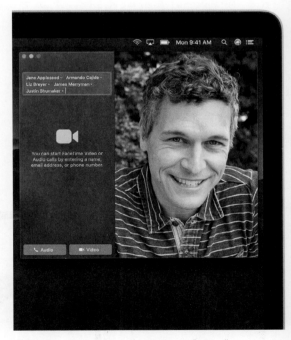

Alternative Text And Video Chat

While Messages and FaceTime are great free tools, they're rather exclusive. If you have friends on PCs and Android phones you wish to text/video chat with, you'll have to download and install Skype (www.skype.com/mac), or try Google hangouts (google.com/chat/video).

Above: Once you have accepted an incoming call, you will be able to see the other user and chat to them.

STAYING PRODUCTIVE ON YOUR MAC

As tempting as it is to spend all day browsing the Internet and FaceTiming with friends, we bought a Mac to get some serious work done. In this section we'll introduce you to the available tools.

THE iWORK SUITE

If you're an experienced PC user (or have at least used one), you'll be familiar with Microsoft Office, which features Word, Excel and PowerPoint. iWork is Apple's answer to Microsoft Office and is free with all new Macs.

What's In iWork?

There are three key apps within iWork. They are Pages, Numbers and Keynote.

- **Pages**: Allows you to create, save and share word-processed documents. As well as those blank documents, you can also fashion attractive flyers and posters, business cards, résumés, letters and more from elegant templates. Compared to Microsoft Word it is quite a simplified, pared-down option.

- **Numbers**: The Apple-made equivalent of Microsoft Excel. This spreadsheet creation tool is capable of so much more. It enables users to create attractive, easy-to-follow charts and reports to brighten up those numbers.

- **Keynote**: Apple's interpretation of Microsoft PowerPoint, it helps you to create good-looking office presentations, which actually stand some chance of capturing your audience's attention.

Inside An iWork App: Pages

As each of these apps could probably demand a chapter in this book, we're just going to take a closer look at Pages here, as all three apps operate on quite similar principles.

To start work within Pages, find it in your Applications folder and open the app. You'll be greeted with the Choose A Template screen. Select Blank Document.

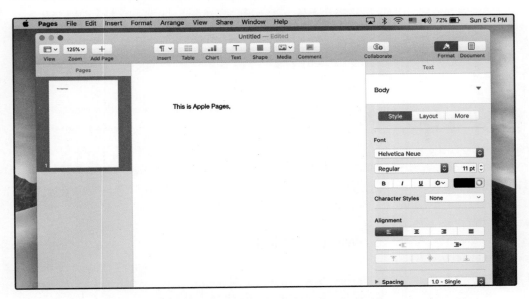

Above: Pages is the document program within iWork. To start a new document, simply select Blank Document and start typing.

Immediately, you can begin typing within the app.

1. To add the Charts, Tables, Shapes and Media (this includes music and video), use the relevant items in the toolbar.

2. To use the Format sidebar to change the look and appearance of text, select the text in question and choose options from the font, size, colour, spacing, style and alignment options.

3. Hit the View section of the toolbar to customize what options and thumbnails you see within the window.

4. To save progress, hit Command + S, choose a filename and a destination. The default location is within your iCloud folder.

5. You can hit the Collaborate button to work with fellow iCloud users in real time if your colleagues or friends are also iCloud users. This button will allow you to send a link to the file so they can edit. All changes will be saved back to the document.

> **Hot Tip**
>
> You can quit iWork apps without saving and not have to worry about losing your work. The app autosaves and re-opens in the last place you left it. We'd still save to be on the safe side though!

> **Hot Tip**
>
> Collaboration is the key for iWork in iCloud. When working within the browser, you can copy the link and share it with fellow iCloud users. Anyone with an Apple ID can now work on the document.

Alternatives To iWork

If you don't have free iWork, the apps can be downloaded from the Mac App Store relatively cheaply. However, there are ways to access productivity apps without forking out more money. Notes (see page 113) and TextEdit are built in apps that allow you to get down your thoughts. However, there's also iWork for iCloud.

iWork In iCloud

Another 2013 addition, iWork in iCloud allows everyone with an Apple ID to use web-based versions of Pages, Numbers and Keynotes and save them in the iCloud. Head to iCloud.com and sign in using

Hot Tip

Rather than buying iWork apps, you may wish to consider Microsoft Office for Mac. Go to Office.com/Mac for information on how to download the old faithful.

Above: If you prefer Microsoft Office, you can download this for your Mac.

your Apple ID and you'll see access to those apps on your homepage. If you have iWork on your computer, then iWork in iCloud becomes a more important tool. The latest versions of all of your documents will be synced across all of your devices automatically and stored safely in the iCloud. If you've been working on a spreadsheet on your Mac and switch computers, you can pick up where you left off by logging into iCloud, even if you're using a Windows PC.

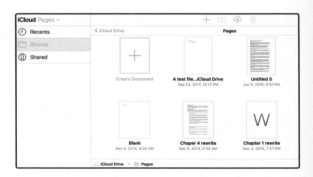

Above: iCloud syncs your iWork documents across all your devices.

Saving To And Opening From iCloud

You can automatically save a document, spreadsheet or presentation to iCloud by hitting Save and selecting iCloud as a destination. All documents saved in iCloud can be opened by selecting Open from the menu and selecting iCloud. These will be the most recent versions.

Above: Open documents saved to iCloud for the most recent version.

ORGANIZING YOUR LIFE

Your Mac is a great tool for work and play, but knowing that you may need a little help co-ordinating your hectic lifestyle, macOS also features a host of tools to help you stay on top of where you need to be and what you need to be doing.

CALENDAR

The macOS calendar is a very underrated feature. It's a massively helpful tool that works across apps, devices, accounts, social networks and syncs everything automatically. Open it up from the dock and your Applications folder.

Above: Events in the Calendar window are colour coded according to where the information is sourced from.

The Calendar Window

When you open the Calendar, you can choose to view the day, week, month or year. Events from different calendar accounts are colour-coded. Clicking them will reveal more information about said event.

Adding An Event

The quickest way to schedule an event in the Calendar app is simply to press the plus button in the window and type in what you're doing. For example, 'Coffee with Karen at 7pm on Friday'. This will immediately add it to the calendar.

Above: To add an event, press the plus button and type in the details.

Adding Accounts
To Your Calendar

It is likely that any Internet accounts (check within System Preferences) you've already set up, such as your Apple ID and email accounts, are also pulling information into the Calendar. You can add others by heading to Calendar > Preferences > Accounts and following the same procedure outlined on page 94 in the Mail section.

Syncing Calendars

Once you've set up your Calendar, you can take comfort in the knowledge that all events will be synced back to that account across all devices. So, if you add an event to your iCloud calendar it'll appear on your Mac, iPhone, iPad and at iCloud.com. Likewise an event set up on your iPhone will be synced back to your Mac. If you add an event to your Gmail calendar from your Mac, it'll show up in your Google Calendar on the web. Thanks iCloud, you're a real pal.

Hot Tip

If you enabled Siri during set-up, it will suggest events to add to your calendar based on items from your Mail account, such as flights and hotel bookings.

Calendar/Mail Integration

The Calendar app plays really nicely with the Mail app: if someone sends you an email saying, for example, let's meet at 1pm on Thursday, you can click this text to add a Calendar event for that time, for which you'll then receive a reminder. This also works for other dates and times that appear within emails, such as travel arrangements and ticket purchase confirmation emails.

Above: You can click a time or date in an email message to add the event to the Calendar app.

Sending Invites

As well as receiving invites through Mail, you can also send them on. Just set up an event in the Calendar. Double click it and begin typing invitees. You can add a full email address and existing contacts will be auto filled in. Send the invite. Once it has been accepted or declined, you'll receive an email.

Calendar Alerts

A digital calendar wouldn't be much use if it didn't give you fair warning of what's coming up. You can head to Calendar > Preferences > Alerts to configure when you get these alerts and how they appear. They also appear in the Notifications Center (see page 115), allowing you to view events at any time, without heading to the Calendar app.

Above: Set up alerts to remind you of calendar events.

REMINDERS, CONTACTS, NOTES, STICKIES, DASHBOARD

While the Calendar app will alert you to appointments, for the basic day-to-day Honeydos (you know, 'honey do this, honey do that') the Reminders app comes in very handy.

Above: Use Reminders for day-to-day things.

Setting Reminders And Ticking Them Off

Reminders is another of those apps that, thanks to iCloud, plays nicely with iOS devices and iCloud.com, so you can set reminders on your Mac and then go around ticking them off on your iPhone (if you have one) or other computer. To set Reminders, open the app from your Applications folder.

1. In the Today pane, hit the + icon and begin typing. Once you've written the text press + again to add further items.

2. To set Reminders for a time or location, hit the 'i' icon next to the list item, select the date and time or the location. The latter will send you a reminder when your computer notices you're at a certain place.

3. To tick off items, tick the box to the left of the text, to push them into the Completed section.

Notes

The Notes app is different to TextEdit and Pages as it's more for your random musings and thoughts than anything else. Here you can jot down anything you wish, add pictures and

> ## Hot Tip
> To ensure items are being synced across macOS and iOS devices, make sure you're adding Reminders under the iCloud pane rather than On My Mac. The latter just works locally.

Above: The Notes app is perfect for random musings and collecting pictures.

other attachments and they'll be stored on your Mac. If you add Notes to your iCloud preferences, they'll also be synced to your other devices and available at iCloud.com. To add to Notes, open the app, hit the + to create a new note and simply begin typing. Everything is saved and synced automatically.

The Notes app also benefits from the new Continuity Camera feature we explained in Mail (*see* page 98). This makes it easy to add photos directly from your iPhone's camera lens to a notes page. You can also collaborate with other users by selecting the Collaborate icon in the toolbar (a person with a + icon). This will allow you to share via other apps or copy the link

Above: Stickies are like virtual sticky notes.

Stickies
Are you the type to leave sticky notes all over your desk at work? Then you'll love the Mac equivalent: Stickies. It's like Notes, but sits nicely on your desktop as a constant reminder of a phone number, activity or email address.

YOUR CONTACTS BOOK
It may be that you seldom open the Address Book app on your Mac, but the presence of those contacts underpins other apps like Mail, Messages, Calendar and more.

Above: Add the details for a new contact.

Importing Contacts
You can add contacts manually. That's cool. However, your other Internet accounts are probably loaded with information. In System Preferences > Internet Accounts, browse through your accounts and check the Contacts tick box to pull everything in. This will bring in Google, Microsoft, Facebook, Twitter accounts and more, plus any contacts you've synced to iCloud.

Adding A New Contact
If you'd like to manually add a new contact, open the app and use the keyboard shortcut Command + N to load a blank card. Type in their vital statistics using the tab key to move between fields.

Acting Upon Contacts
To interact with a contact, tap the indicator next to their phone number/email address and select from the actions. You can email, call through FaceTime, send messages and more.

NOTIFICATIONS CENTER AND ALERTS
The Notifications Center is another relatively new addition to macOS. It's one of those useful features that you forget is there. You can access it by tapping the list icon in the top right corner of the menu bar.

What's In The Notifications Center?
Anything that sends you updates, events or messages; your recent emails, available App Store updates, Skype messages, website updates, newly published articles in the News app, Calendar events and so on. You can configure exactly what you'll be notified about, and how you'll be notified by heading to System Preferences > Notifications.

Alerts
Also within System Preferences > Notifications, you can configure how the alerts appear within the top right corner for each and every app. For example, if you select Mail, you can choose to have no alert, you can choose a banner, which will fade after a couple of seconds, or an alert that requires your attention before it goes away.

Above: The Notification Center contains messages and updates from your apps.

Left: Do Not Disturb settings will keep you free from distracting notifications while you focus.

Other options include showing notifications on the lock screen, showing message previews and playing a sound along with the notification. Play around and see what works for you.

Getting Some Peace And Quiet

Sometimes, you don't want emails, messages, calendar notifications and more flooding your desktop. So Apple has a helpful Do Not Disturb mode within Notifications Center. It's not easy to find. Open the Notification Centre and swipe the trackpad downwards with two fingers. Here you'll see controls for Do Not Disturb and Night Shift. You can further customize the Do Not Disturb settings in System Preferences > Notifications.

FINDING YOUR WAY AROUND IN MAPS

The Apple Maps app from iPhone and iPad has been present in macOS for a number of years now and it sure does look pretty. It's also great for finding directions to friends' houses, meetings, restaurants and everything in between.

Above: The Maps app makes it easy to share your location.

The View From Up High

There are three ways to view Maps in the app: The Map interface shows a graphical representation with place names, Transport shows public transport links and Satellite shows the real deal from those little gadgets in orbit. You'll see these options on the right of the toolbar.

Where Am I?

You can navigate directly to your current location by hitting the compass arrow in the top left corner.

Getting Directions With Your Mac

The primary purpose of this app is to assist users in finding their way from A to B. Maps will provide you with detailed turn-by-turn route information, which you can share with other people, print off, or even send directly to the Maps app on your iPhone before you set off. Here's how to get those directions.

Step 3: Enter start and end locations, then press Enter to load directions.

1. Hit the Search bar in the centre of the window and type in the name or address of your destination. When it appears in the drop-down options, click it.

2. Hit Directions in the toolbar to load the address as your end point. If you have location settings available, your current location will load as the start point.

3. If you're choosing a different starting point, type this in to the Start field and select from the drop down menu.

4. Use the indicators to toggle between walking, driving and transit directions.

Sharing Locations And Directions

Within Maps it's possible to share your location or directions through Mail, Messages, Notes, Reminders, AirDrop to another user and more. This feature is really helpful in a number of ways.

- **Share directions via email and messages**: Plot a route for friends and family to follow that they can print off on their journey.

- **Email to yourself**: Print off the PDF and use it on the road.

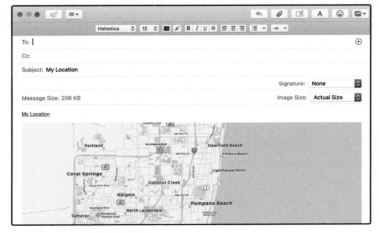

Above: You can send the directions in an email for others to print and use.

- **Send to iOS**: A great feature that allows you to send the directions you've just plotted to another device where they can be followed along the journey with voice-powered turn-by-turn navigation assistance.

- **Add to Favourites**: If this is a journey you plan to make a number of times, you can select the heart icon from the share menu.

Points Of Interest

Maps is also useful for finding places to visit in your local area. Simply click on a place of interest to get contact information and even reviews from Yelp.com.

Hot Tip

In selected cities you can use the Flyover tool, which allows you to tour famous cities from the comfort of your office chair. Where Flyover is available you can zoom in and hit the 3D icon in the toolbar. Then use multi-touch gestures (two fingers on the trackpad to pan, pinch to zoom) to navigate the skyline.

WHAT'S ON YOUR DASHBOARD?

We've mentioned the Mac dashboard a couple of times but haven't delved in yet. The dashboard is filled with useful widgets like a mini calendar, a calculator, a weather forecast, currency converter and more. It's perfect for times when you don't need a full application.

How To Access It

Where is this mysterious dashboard then? Well, it has its own area of the OS away from everything else. You can select Mission Control (see page 78) and then choose dashboard, or you can access it through a multi-touch gesture. We use a left swipe with four fingers to move to the dashboard. This can be configured in trackpad preferences.

Customizing To The Dashboard

On your dashboard you'll see the widgets mentioned above, but you can add more by clicking the + icon and delete others using the – button. You can add flight trackers, world clocks, local cinema screenings and more.

Above: The dashboard contains a multitude of useful widgets.

Hot Tip
You can easily move widgets around the dashboard by picking them up and dragging them to a new destination.

Above: Customize the dashboard by adding other widgets.

IMPORTING AND WORKING WITH YOUR PHOTOS

Before you go sharing photographs and videos, you've got to get them on to your Mac. Thankfully it's really simple to import media from your camera and keep those special memories safe.

PHOTOS

Whether they're taken on your iPhone or on your standalone camera, the Photos app looks after your precious photos. It comes built into all Macs and is represented by the colorful petal icon in the dock.

Importing Your Pictures

There's nothing worse than losing/breaking a memory card packed with holiday snaps that can never be replaced, so it's important that you import photos at the earliest opportunity. Photos makes it easy.

1. Once you plug in your digital camera or mobile device, either via the USB cable or by removing the memory card and plugging it into your Mac (either with a memory card adapter or through the built-in SD card slot), Photos should begin bouncing in the dock and open. If it does not open automatically, click the Photos app to open manually.

2. Immediately, you'll see all photos on the card/camera load on to an import screen within the app. The camera will appear under Devices in the sidebar within Photos.

3. Select each of the photos you wish to import (remember what we said about batch selecting items on page 65) and hit Import Selected. Alternatively, you can just import everything. If you've used this memory card before, Photos will also give you the opportunity to Import All New Items.

Step 5: Once you have imported the selected photos, they will remain on your Mac's hard drive.

4. Once the upload is complete, Photos will ask if you want to keep or delete the imported photos from your memory card. Unless your card is filling up, keep them for now.

5. Next you'll be taken straight to the Import page, and your photos now reside on your Mac's hard drive.

6. Browse to Photos in the Library section, scroll to the newest batch, click the title and type in a name.

Other Import Options

If you have photos on your phone or perhaps some lying around your computer and you want to bring them into the Photos fold, it's pretty straightforward. Select File > Import to Library (Command + Shift + I) and browse to the files of your choosing within the pop-up dialogue box.

Browsing With Photos

There's so much you can do within Photos. Double click any of the thumbnail photos and it will fill the window. Here you can do the following.

- **Give it a name!:** Select the 'i' button to change from the original file name to add your own title. This will make it easier to find in future.

- **Add a description:** See above.

- **Favourites:** Particularly proud of an image? Tap the heart button to add it to a list of favourites.

- **Zoom:** Want a closer look at a certain aspect of the photo? Use the zoom scroller in the left corner of the Photos window. You'll see a little Navigation tab pop up, which lets you know where you are in the photo.

Above: Apple Photos has adequate editing tools for you to touch up your photo before adding to an album or sharing.

- **Edit it:** Click Edit at the bottom right corner of the window to load the options. There are loads of Quick Fixes to get rid of red-eye, crop unwanted elements, rotate, straighten and more. You can also click Effects to add filters like Sepia, or Black and White. The Adjust tab lets you get into some more advanced colour level editing.

- **Auto enhance**: If you don't want to spend time editing, hitting the wand in the toolbar is a smart way to adjust colours, contrast and brightness automatically.

Working With Photos

Lets say, just for argument's sake, that all of your snaps are now sitting comfortably within Photos, perfectly organized into events and albums. (Hey! We can dream, can't we?) What else can we do?

- **Merge Albums**: Drag and drop one Album from the list onto another.

- **Faces**: Select the Faces tab in the sidebar to see pictures of individuals within your albums. Select Find Faces to add more and soon, Photos will begin to recognise familiar faces and suggest tags.

- **Places**: Mobile photos are sometimes geo-tagged, allowing you to hit Places to view where they were taken on a map.

- **Search**: In the top right corner, tap search and type in names, keywords, locations, event names and more.

Sharing From Photos

One good thing about using Photos to store all of your digital camera and mobile photos all in one place is the one-stop-shop sharing options it provides. If you so desire, you can share single photos or entire albums directly to Facebook. Other options include sharing photos or an entire album to Mail, Messages, Notes and iCloud Shared Albums. Hit the Share button in the top right corner and follow the on-screen instructions.

Be careful not to email too many photos at a time, as most providers have an attachment limit. Gmail for example is 25 MB, which is about 10 hi-res photos. This is where iCloud Shared Albums comes in handy. It will upload the photos to iCloud and provide recipients with a link to access them, or send them a notification to their iPhone. From there, they too will be able to add to the album.

CREATING PHOTO ALBUMS

Importing new photos will automatically create date-based Events within Photos. You may also wish to create custom albums bringing memories together. This is super simple.

1. First select an Event in the sidebar: hit Command + N and a new 'untitled album' will appear beneath Albums in the sidebar featuring all of those photos. Type in a name of your choice.
2. To create a brand new empty album, select Photos from the sidebar and hit Command + N. Give it a name.

Above: Sort your photos into different albums. Create new albums and give them names.

Above: iCloud Shared Albums enables your friends and family to access and add to photo albums.

3. To add photos to a new or existing album, select the pictures of your choice and drag and drop them on to the album name. Alternatively, select the photos and use the right click on them. Then select Add To in the bottom right and choose the album.

PHOTOSTREAMS AND iCLOUD

We're afraid this is one of those points where this book only becomes useful for those who are into Apple beyond their Mac computer. If you're an iPhone owner (please don't take photos on your

> ### Hot Tip
> To send all new photos taken on your camera directly to your iCloud PhotoStream, select Photos in the menu bar, click Preferences > iCloud and tick the relevant box.

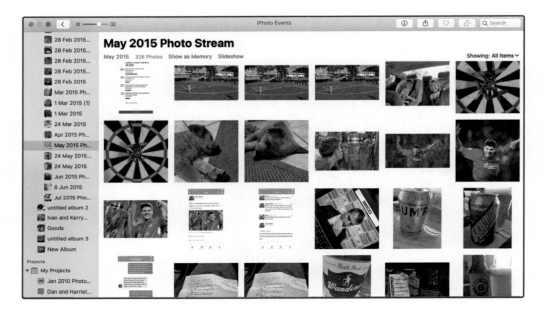

Above: Photos taken on an iPhone will be automatically uploaded to your PhotoStream via iCloud.

iPad – it looks very silly), iCloud will safeguard photos taken on your phone, automatically uploading up to 1,000 of them to your PhotoStream. Photos will download them from the cloud and place them in monthly albums so they can hang out on your computer. Here they can be browsed, edited and shared or simply remain for safekeeping.

To ensure Photos is configured with iCloud, go to Internet Accounts, select iCloud and tick the Photos option.

OTHER PHOTO TOOLS

Photos is the best way to mange your library on your Mac, but there are loads of other tools that allow you to view and even take photos quickly and easily. There are also tons of additional software you can download.

Quick Look

The quickest way to see a photo that's saved to your Mac is the aptly named Quick Look tool. Right click on an image file and select Quick Look to instantly see the photo, or simply hit the space bar. It's great for identifying small thumbnails without opening the image. From here you can close (Command + W), share elsewhere (*see page 123*) or open in Preview.

Preview

The Preview app is the bridge between Quick Look and Photos. Double click most images and they'll open in Preview by default. You can zoom, rotate, annotate, share and save elsewhere, but not a lot else. It also opens PDFs and other documents.

Above: Most images will automatically open in Preview, for a quick look.

Photo Booth

If you want to take self-portraits on your Mac and add fun effects you can use Photo Booth. Open the app from Utilities and create a Photo Booth Library. Your iSight camera will kick in and you can hit the red capture button to take a picture. You can choose to take four photos at once, or record video messages you can share. Hit effects to browse through a host of zany options to distort, contort and discolour your features. Photo Booth is also the default app loaded when you're choosing a new profile picture for your Mac.

Above: Add fun effects to photos with Photo Booth.

MORE BUILT-IN MAC APPS

We'll go into more detail about these apps throughout the book. For example, we deal with iTunes in the Entertainment Chapter and Photos over the next new pages. However, there are some more built-in apps worthy of a mention right here.

News

A new (get it) addition on Mac, the news app has been brought over from iPhone and iPad. It brings together all content from all of your favourite news sources and learns as you read. The idea is a constantly-updating digest that brings the best of the web to your desktop in one place.

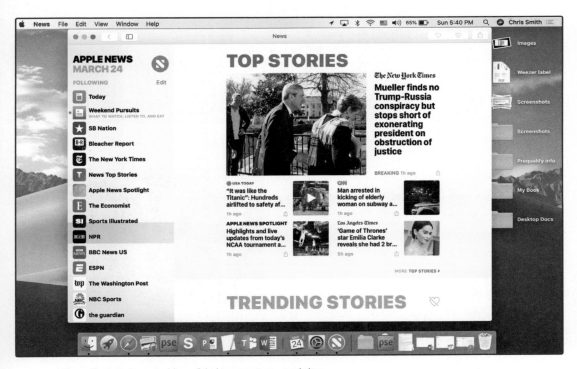

Above: The Apple News app delivers all the biggest stories to your desktop.

Above: The Apple Home app will allow you to control any HomeKit enabled lights, locks, switches and more.

Home

If you have smart home equipment like lights, plugs, blinds, speakers, switches, air-conditioners, you can control these from your Mac using the Home app. This is an advanced feature, but if you're looking to start a smart home, look for the Works With Apple HomeKit symbol on the aforementioned products.

Siri

We mentioned Siri in set-up. The app has also made it over from iPhone and iPad and lets you use your voice to find answers. If you enabled it during set-up, you're good to go. If you skipped, head to System Preferences > Siri. To summon Siri:

1. Hold Command + Space

2. Tap the Siri icon in the menu bar

3. Select the Siri icon from the Dock

4. 2018/2019 Macs offer 'Hey Siri' hand-free voice controls, which enable you to simply say 'Hey Siri' to summon the assistant.

What You Can Ask Siri

Siri enables Mac users to perform a large number of tasks, pertaining to a wide range of apps. Here are some of the commands Apple recommends:

- 'Show the PDFs in my Downloads folder.'
- 'How much free space do I have on my Mac?'
- 'Play the top 40 jazz songs.'
- 'What's the weather in Lake Tahoe?'
- 'Find tweets from José Bautista.'
- 'Search the web for images of the Eiffel Tower.'
- 'Show me all of the files I shared with Cecilia last week.'
- 'FaceTime Victoria.'
- 'Add Laura to my 10 AM meeting.'
- 'Show my photos from yesterday.'
- 'What time is it in Monterrey, Mexico?'
- 'Find coffee near me.'

Right: Siri is relatively new to the Mac and allows us to make voice commands.

How is the weather today

Nice weather coming up today... up to 82°F:

WEATHER

Pompano Beach

Partly Cloudy
Chance of Rain: 20%
High: 82° Low: 66°

78°

Now	7PM	7:34PM	8PM	9PM
78°	79°	Sunset	75°	75°

Monday	20%	82°	66°
Tuesday	20%	84°	63°
Wednesday	20%	79°	64°
Thursday	20%	75°	70°
Friday	40%	79°	70°

INSTALLING NEW APPS

By now you should have a pretty good grasp of what your Mac is capable of out of the box, but there's so much more to enjoy. In this section we'll guide you through finding additional apps, downloading and installing them.

FINDING NEW APPS

There are loads of apps you may have used on your PC that you'd like to bring into the fold on your Mac. Usually that's not a problem, as there are very few apps that don't have a Mac-based version these days. If you head to page 252, you'll find hundreds of 'em. Primarily you'll obtain these apps by two means – either the Mac App Store or by downloading them via the Internet.

Hot Tip

The Mac App Store doesn't have everything, but when downloading from here you'll know that the software has been approved and tested by Apple.

THE MAC APP STORE

Following the success of the iOS App Store, Apple decided to introduce one for the Mac. Previously software was mostly downloaded through the browser or through physical media like pocket hard drives and CDs. In the digital age, you can have the software up and running on your Mac in minutes.

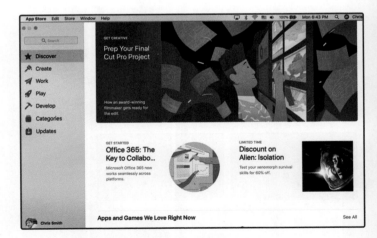

Above: Visit the Mac App store to download new software.

Using The Mac App Store

To open the Store click the 'A' icon in the dock or select the Apple logo in the menu bar and select App Store. Here you'll be able to browse between tabs for Discover, Create, Work, Play and Categories Featured (apps Apple is promoting), Charts, Categories (Business, Entertainment, Productivity, Social Media, Education, etc.), and Updates showing new versions of any of the apps you own.

Searching For Apps

If you don't have a specific app in mind, but are looking for something to fulfil a specific need, let's say a Twitter client for your Mac, the easiest way is to Select Categories > Social Networking. This will show you a list of available apps, but also, on the right side of the window you'll see the Top Free and Top Paid apps, keying you into what's popular with other users.

Hot Tip

Keep your eye on the Discover tab, as it offers a good selection of brand-new apps and games as well as Editor's Choices and specially grouped collections like Big Name Games.

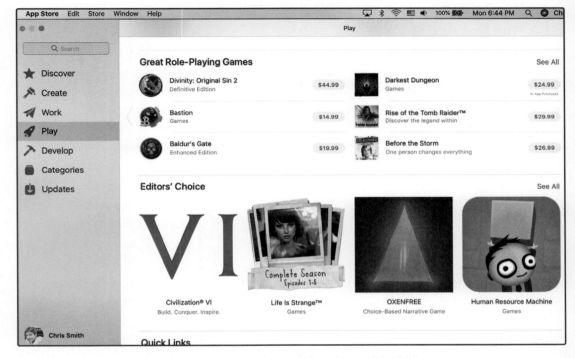

Above: The Mac App Store promotes and suggests certain apps to help you find something worth downloading.

If you know what you want, simply type the name into the Search bar. If that app is available within the store, it will come up in the search results. If not, see the section on downloading apps from the Internet (page 134).

Downloading From The Mac App Store

Once you've found the app, hit the Get/Price icon attached to each app logo and then Install/Buy app. You'll need to enter your Apple ID password to sign in. If you still haven't created an Apple ID (come on, you really should have by now!), you can do so here. Once you've signed in, the download will begin. You'll see the progress in the Launchpad icon within the dock.

Installing Apps From The Mac App Store

This part is going to be short and sweet. One of the advantages of downloading from the App Store is all of the installation stuff is handled for you. Once a download is complete, head to the app in Launchpad. It'll have a blue dot next to it. Click to open. You may have to agree to some Ts & Cs, but that's it. You're ready to start using it.

Hot Tip
Some app updates require you to restart your computer in order for them to take effect. Make sure everything is saved before you do.

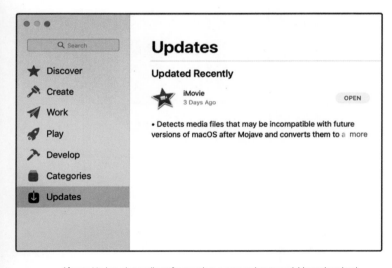

Above: Update alerts will notify you when a new update is available to download.

Updating Apps

Another advantage (they're starting to rack up aren't they?) is the App Store notification when a new version of the app is available to download. You can see Updates within the App Store itself, but you'll also get an alert as soon as an update is available. Clicking this alert opens the App Store, allowing you to update to new versions of apps.

FINDING APPLICATIONS ONLINE

There are loads and loads of popular apps that play perfectly nicely with your Mac but don't feature on the Mac App Store. Apps we've mentioned in this chapter, in fact. Spotify isn't there, Skype isn't there, Google Chrome isn't there and Firefox isn't there. You'll need to go online to get them.

1. Open your Internet browser and type the name of the program into the search bar; for example, 'Skype for Mac'.

2. From the search results, pick the top couple of results as they'll be the most official portals and it'll likely take you straight to where you need to be.

3. Follow the on-screen instructions (you may have to enter details and spend some money before you download) to begin the download.

4. Depending on which browser you use, the download take place in different areas. In Safari, it's to the right of the URL bar. The progress will be depicted by the blue progress bar.

5. Once the download is complete, double click the file from within the Downloads list in Safari.

6. The install file (usually with a .dmg suffix) will begin to unpack and you'll see the app in Finder.

7. Usually, you'll be asked to drag the icon into the Applications folder.

8. Browse to the Applications folder and double click as you usually would. The first time you open you'll be asked whether you trust the web program. Hit open and you're good to go.

Step 7: Drag the icon into the Applications folder when indicated on screen.

ENTERTAINMENT

iTUNES

An application so famous, influential and functional it could fill a book all by itself, iTunes houses your music, movies, TV shows, podcasts, audiobooks and enables you to play them back. It also allows you to purchase content from the iTunes Store or subscribe to Apple Music where you can stream all of the world's music for a monthly fee.

iTUNES MUSIC AND VIDEO

iTunes started off as a music portal (hence the name). Like Photos it's a great media library, allowing music to be accessed and played back quickly and easily. Later, we'll talk about buying music and video and streaming from the Apple Music subscription service, but for now let's focus on playback.

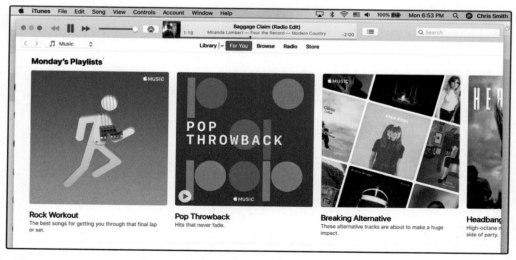

Above: iTunes can be opened by clicking the colourful musical note icon in the dock.

Above: There are a number of ways to import music into your iTunes music library.

Getting Your Files On To iTunes

Open up iTunes by clicking the blue musical note in the dock. What do you see? An empty library. To change this you'll need to get your music on to your Mac. There are a number of ways to do this.

- **Import from hard drive:** If you already have a digital music collection from another PC, then it's easy to bring it into iTunes, providing you've transferred it to a hard drive that can be plugged into your Mac (see page 33). Browse to the files or folders you wish to import, drag them and drop them on the iTunes logo or within the app itself. Alternatively, hit Command + O in iTunes to find them.

- **Import from CD:** If your Mac has a disc drive or you have an external accessory, you can import your entire CD collection. Music CDs automatically open in iTunes. Simply click Import and the entire CD will be added to your digital library.

- **Download from iCloud:** If you've purchased music and video from iTunes before using your Apple ID on another computer or mobile device, it can be downloaded freely on to your Mac (see page 143).

iTunes Playback

Now you've actually got some music and videos to play. Hooray. From here it's all pretty smooth sailing in terms of playback. Just double click a song to get started. Let's take a quick look at the iTunes control system.

- **Play/Pause:** Well, this one, you know, plays and pauses stuff. Space bar for pausing and playing also works pretty well here, as do the keyboard's media controls.

Above: Click the skip arrows to move to the next or previous file.

Above: The progress bar shows how much time is left.

Above: Type in a particular term to search the library.

- **Skip arrows:** Tap these to move to the next file, hold them to scan backwards and forwards.

- **Volume:** Drag the scroll bar back and forth.

- **AirPlay:** Providing another AirPlay device is on the same Wi-Fi network, you can send the content to speakers, or another display (see page 172).

- **Mini player:** Simplified playback controls.

- **Album artwork:** Load the mini-player.

- **Shuffle:** Play items in a random order.

- **Now playing:** Click the three dots to load options like add to playlist, go to artist.

- **Progress bar:** Shows how long has passed and how long is left. Can be clicked or dragged to different sections.

◯ **Repeat**: Press once to repeat an album/playlist, twice to repeat the current item.

◯ **List**: Shows the songs coming up next. Can be selected from the list.

◯ **Search**: Search library. Click within the field and begin typing.

◯ **Full screen**: Take your iTunes experience to the max by pressing the green circle.

Above: The Library drop-down menu allows you to switch between types of media.

◯ **Library**: Switch between the music, TV shows and movies you have stored on your computer. Each type of media offers different options. For example, Music allows you to switch between songs, albums, artists and more.

◯ **Devices**: If an iPhone, iPod or iPad is connected via a USB cable or you have synced it to connect over Wi-Fi, it will appear on the right side.

Hot Tip
If you want to sync your iPhone over Wi-Fi, plug in to your Mac via USB. Open the phone from the toolbar, select Summary, browse to options and tick Sync this iPhone over Wi-Fi.

THE iTUNES STORE

You thought the free software and free Beats Radio station was out of the kindness of Apple's heart? No! They just want you to splash the cash on buying music and video from iTunes or streaming music from Apple Music. We'll deal with the former first.

WHAT'S IN THE iTUNES STORE?

This is your one-stop shop for digital media. It's sitting right within your computer and everything is available to you right now. Whether you want to buy albums and singles, rent or buy films, everything is here.

iTUNES STORE HOMEPAGE

From the iTunes homepage, you can hit the Store button below the playbar to enter the store. From here you can click Music, Films, TV Programmes, Podcasts or Audiobooks from the drop down menu on the left of the toolbar. Depending on which department of the store you're in, you'll see a wide range of content. For example, the music section shows new and featured albums, charts, offers, pre-order items and more. For films, you'll see a similar array of content.

Right: Singles, albums, movies, TV shows and podcasts and audiobooks are all available from the iTunes Store.

Finding What You Want

If you see something that tickles your fancy on the homepage, click it, hit Buy, enter your Apple ID, username and password, and agree to purchase. Otherwise, type your desired album, movie or TV show into the search bar.

Downloading

Any purchases you make on the iTunes Store are yours to keep for ever. As soon as you hit that Buy

Above: You can search for a particular artist to see a list of all their available songs.

button, the download will start. You can keep track of it in the Now Playing pane, and as soon as individual items finish downloading, they'll be available in your library.

Using iCloud To Reinstate Purchases

Another way to get music/video you own on to your Mac is to re-download stuff you've already purchased from iTunes. It's easy to do through the iTunes Store. On the storefront, hit Purchased and then the iCloud icon next to the purchase items to add them to your Mac library.

Renting Or Buying?

Most things on the iTunes Store are yours to keep and can be transported and re-downloaded to multiple devices until the end of time. This is the case for TV

Left: It is possible to re-download already purchased items.

shows, music videos, albums, singles, books, apps and whatever else. However, there is also an option to rent movies.

While it's not available for all movies, on some films (especially new releases) you can select the option to rent for much less than it costs to buy. This will allow you to watch the movie any time in the next 30 days.

Once you start watching, you have 48 hours to finish the movie. In that 48 hours you can watch it as many times as you like, but once it expires it will disappear from your hard drive.

iTunes Radio

It's not all about buying music from the iTunes Store (*see page 142*) anymore. Apple offers an Apple Music subscription service, which we'll explain in a second. However, there's another way to stream music through iTunes. The Radio section enables you to freely listen to news and sports radio and Apple's own Beats 1 radio station, which runs 24/7. Simply browse to a station of your choosing and hit play to begin.

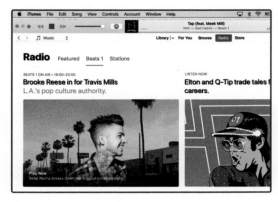

However, to listen to custom-build stations based on genres, currently charting hits and to build your own radio stations, you'll need to sign up for Apple Music.

Above: Apple's Beats 1 radio station is free to air and runs 24/7.

APPLE MUSIC

If you buy more than one album a month, the Apple Music subscription service provides much better value for money. For £9.99/$9.99 a month you get unlimited access to 50 million songs as opposed to just 12–13. You can stream them online or save them to your devices for offline playback. It offers countless hand-built playlists and you can even fashion your own radio stations.

Signing Up For Apple Music

Apple will give you a completely free month of Apple Music to take all of those benefits for a spin. You've probably seen the invites posted all over iTunes. Select one of the banners or select the For You and Browse tabs beneath the playbar. Here you'll be asked to input your Apple ID username and password in order to sign up for the trial. After a month you'll be charged £9.99/$9.99 a month, unless you cancel, which you can do at any time. If you cancel before the end of the one month trial you will not be charged.

Using Apple Music

Once you're signed up, you'll be asked to choose genres and bands to help Apple make recommendations. From there you're like Charlie with the key to the proverbial Chocolate Factory.

- **For You**: This will show personalised selections, based on your listening history and identified tastes.

- **Browse**: Here you can examine a wider selection of what's on offer. You'll also see charts, hand-crafted playlists and much more.

- **Radio**: Once you're subscribed to Apple Music, the Radio section of iTunes opens up, allowing you to access genre-based Radio stations.

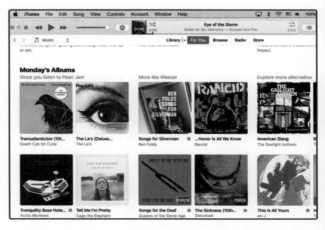

Above: The For You section of Apple Music provides you with bespoke playlists, recommendations and much more.

○ **Search**: If there's something particular you're looking for, just search for it. Now you won't be asked to buy it, you can just play it.

Playing With Apple Music

As with iTunes, clicking on the play button begins the playback, and all of the playback controls we learned earlier in the chapter still apply. You can also add content to your main iTunes library and download it so you can play it when you're away from the Internet.

○ **Add**: If you see the word 'Add' or the + symbol, tap this to add a piece of content to your Library where it can be easily accessed and will sit alongside other content you've downloaded and imported.

○ **Download:**
Hit the iCloud button to download it to your Mac. As long as you're subscribed to Apple Music, you will have access to this content.

Hot Tip

To create a custom Station from a song, artist or album, use the right click (Control+Click) and select Create Station. It will begin a long stream of content from that artist and others in the same wheelhouse.

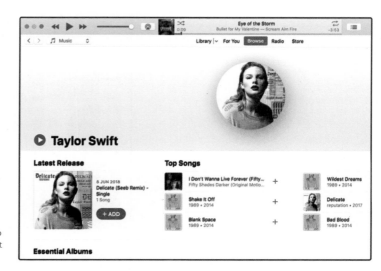

Right: Click the Add (or +) button to add any artist, track, album or playlist to your library.

YOU GOT GAME

Mac computers have never really been regarded highly as gaming devices, but that doesn't mean you can't enjoy some new and classic titles on your computer. Here's how to get gaming.

GAMES ON THE MAC APP STORE

Enter the App Store (see page 131) and go to Play. There you'll find everything from fun, free time-killers to versions of console and PC classics. It's not as well stocked as the iOS App Store, but there's still plenty to keep you entertained.

Downloading Games From The Mac App Store

Nothing really new to see here. You can download and buy games in the same way you do apps from the Mac App Store. There are Featured Games, Top Charts and so on to be found within the store. You can obtain everything from the Call Of Duty games to simple smartphone stuff like Angry Birds.

Controlling Games On Your Mac

All games downloaded through the Mac App Store can be controlled using your mouse/trackpad and keyboard. You can also connect your Mac to a USB or Bluetooth control pad.

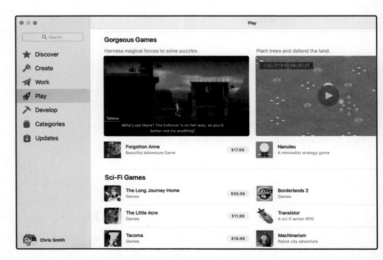

Above: The App Store offers a multitude of games to download.

READING BOOKS

You can also read books on your Mac, with millions of titles available to purchase from Books app, and what's more, all can be synced across your Apple mobile devices.

Above: Access a large library from the Books app.

THE BOOKS APP

This newly introduced app operates in a very similar way to the iTunes Store and the Mac App Store. It gives access to a huge library of new bestsellers and classics that can be immediately obtained and downloaded to your Mac.

Downloading Books

Open the Books app from your Applications folder and sign in using your Apple ID. You'll be shown your book library, which will include those already purchased using your login on other devices. From there it's straightforward. You can see charts, featured titles, bestseller lists and there's the facility to search.

Once you've found your title you can choose to buy the whole book or buy a sample. Usually the publisher grants a sizeable excerpt or the first chapter or two free of charge, or you can

Hot Tip

If you already own an Amazon Kindle reader or have non-Apple mobile devices, you're better off downloading the free, cross-platform Kindle App for your Mac to ensure your purchases are available on all of your devices.

just buy the whole thing straight off. Selecting either option will download it to your Books app.

Free Books

Ebooks can be really, really expensive given you don't get anything physical for your money, but did you know the world is awash with classics you can download for free because the copyright has expired? Enter the Free Books section of Books and you'll see the likes of Sherlock Holmes, *The Wizard Of Oz* and *Pride And Prejudice* available, free of charge.

Reading Books In Books

Reading an entire book on your Mac isn't the greatest experience in all honesty; they're better suited to mobile devices. However, it does work and can be handy if you're working on an essay and need to reference elements of the book. Here are a few basics.

- **Turn pages**: Move the arrow keys left and right.

- **Highlight text**: Hold the mouse/trackpad button down where you want to begin highlighting and drag the trackpad to the end of the section.

- **Copying text**: Hit Command + C.

- **Pasting text in another app**: Command + V.

- **Annotate text**: Highlight section, select Notes from the pop-up window and begin typing.

- **Highlight text**: Highlight the section and choose a colour.

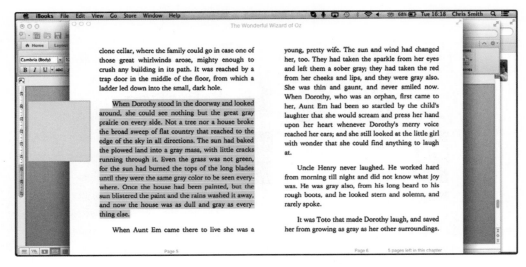

Above: You can use the mouse or trackpad to highlight text. The notepad icon allows you to access these later.

- **Access Notes/Highlights**:
  Click the notepad icon in the toolbar.

- **Look up text**: Highlight text, select More and choose from web, Wikipedia or the rest of the book to load results.

- **Dictionary search**: Double tap on a word.

- **Change font/size/style**: Hit the double A icon in the toolbar.

- **Search for text**: Hit the magnifying class and begin typing in the field.

- **Add bookmarks**: Hitting the bookmark icon in the toolbar turns it red, saving the page. Hitting the drop-down arrow next to it shows all bookmarks.

> ## Hot Tip
> To zoom in and out on text, hit Command along with the plus or minus key on the keyboard.

GETTING CREATIVE WITH YOUR MAC

As we mentioned earlier in the book, the great creative tools are a one of the key motivations for people buying Macs. Right out of the box, your computer comes with some simple yet powerful tools to help you create your own movies and music.

GARAGEBAND

GarageBand is one of the most popular Apple-made apps ever. It allows you to create entire songs on your Mac, complete with percussion, vocals, effects and much more. You don't need to know how to read or play music to create a song. If you can? You can plug your guitar in and record a riff directly on to your Mac.

Above: GarageBand is an incredibly popular app which allows you to make music on your Mac.

iMOVIE

Just as Photos lets you work wonders with your photographs, iMovie allows you to turn your home movies into fully edited projects, complete with audio, effects, captions and more. Then you can share them with family and friends or upload on to YouTube for the whole world to enjoy.

Hot Tip

For more apps for creative types, check out our 100 Top Apps on pages 252–253.

NETWORKING AND SHARING

GETTING ONLINE AT HOME AND IN PUBLIC

It may sound obvious, but your Mac isn't able to magically connect to the Internet without the presence of some external factors. In this section we'll guide you through the complexities of the connected home.

WHAT YOU'LL NEED

As we discussed back at the beginning, each Mac you buy is capable of connecting to wireless and wired Internet networks, but to make that happen at home you'll need a few additional things at your disposal.

Above: You will need a live broadband account in order to connect your Mac to the Internet.

A Live Broadband Account

Unless you have a live account with an Internet provider, such BT, Sky, Virgin, TalkTalk and the like, then you won't be getting on the Internet. These ISPs (Internet service providers) offer contracts at a monthly rate, where you'll be able to select the speed of your connection and the amount of data you'll be allowed to download. The package you choose will depend on mainly two factors.

1. How many devices (tablets, phones, computers, speakers, printers, etc.) do you wish to connect to the network? The more devices, the larger the load the network must cope with.

2. What will you use your connection for? Downloading and streaming lots of media? You'll want faster speeds and potentially unlimited data. Casually browsing the web and sending emails? You can get away with modest speeds and data allowance.

Broadband Equipment

Your Mac has everything inside to connect to the Internet, but wherever you connect there'll need to be some sort of Internet receiver. In the home this usually translates to a wireless broadband modem. This will be supplied by the company you sign up with. You can have them come and install if you wish, or they'll send you the modem with an easy set-up guide. You'll be online and surfing quick as a flash.

Above: Broadband providers will supply a wireless modem when you sign up and can also install it for you.

A Home Phone Landline

While this is not always the case, most ISPs also require you to have a live BT phone line. The exception is Virgin, which offers fibre-optic cable broadband. It is not available in all areas, so check online.

Ethernet Cable

On some models like the iMac and Mac mini you can plug an Internet cable in directly for a wired connection. The Ethernet port that enabled wired Internet has been scarified on all new MacBooks to save space, so you'll need an adapter like the one pictured here. They're £29/$29 from Apple.

Right: An Ethernet adapter.

GETTING ONLINE

Now the home is configured we can jump online. Here's a quick guide to connecting to your home network, if you didn't already do so when setting up your Mac.

CONNECTING WIRELESSLY TO YOUR HOME NETWORK

If you have a live broadband account and a wireless modem (they mostly all are these days), you'll be able to connect to Wi-Fi. All Macs are equipped with Wi-Fi technology that enables easy pairing with a nearby router.

The first step is to identify the name of the network you're connecting to. It'll be identified on your modem as the network ID. Usually it'll consist of the name of your broadband provider together with a combination of letters and numbers (for example BTHomeHub2-HM26).

Step 3: Select the correct network ID from the drop-down menu.

1. Hit the Internet signal icon in your Mac's menu bar. If you're not connected, it'll be empty.

2. If Wi-Fi is noted as Off, turn it On.

3. The list of networks in range will appear in the drop-down menu. Choose the network ID that corresponds with your home network (see above).

4. Enter the password. This will also be given on the modem.

From now on your Mac will remember this and automatically connect to this network whenever you're in range. This enables you to wander around your house without being tethered by wires.

The Importance Of The Password

Ensure you always keep your network password safe and secure to prevent other people (neighbours, perhaps) from jumping on to your network. Password settings can be altered by logging into your modem. Contact your ISP and find out the unique IP address for that modem and type this into your web browser. You'll also need an admin password (it's usually 'admin'). Once you're in, you can change the network password to something stronger, rather than the generic network key shown on the modem.

Staying Wired

If your Mac is likely to stay in one place, like on your desk, then you may want to employ a wired connection to the network. All new Macs have the ability to connect to lightning-fast gigabit Ethernet connections, which means you'll be able to harness the full power of your network speed. As we mentioned above, you may need an adapter to connect. It's also easier to set up and more secure than wireless networks. You can achieve this by using the aforementioned Ethernet cables and plugging them into your Mac and the modem. This should automatically connect you to the network. If not, go to the Troubleshooting section that deals with the Internet on page 212.

Above: The network ID and password will usually be displayed somewhere on the modem; here it is given on the rear of the unit.

Am I Connected?

There are a few ways to check that you're online. The easiest is to open Safari and browse to a webpage. If that page loads, well, it's safe to say you're online. You can also head to System Preferences > Network. If the green light in the sidebar is lit, then you're online. If you see red or amber lights, you may be connected to a network itself, but without access to the Internet. We'll deal with that in the final Troubleshooting chapter (see page 212).

CONNECTING TO A PUBLIC NETWORK WIRELESSLY

If you snapped up a MacBook Air or a MacBook Pro, the chances are you're going to be using it on the go, in the office, at friends' houses, and in cafés and coffee shops around town. Here are a few tips to help you out.

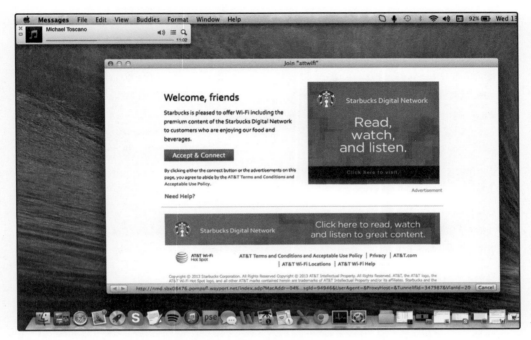

Above: Some public places, such as coffee shops, offer a wireless Internet connection.

Public Networks And Passwords

There are few differences between connecting wirelessly at home and in public. The main difference comes in the password situation. Workplaces and smaller businesses will likely password-protect their networks. In this case you'll need to request the password from the premises' IT guys or the staff with the password.

On other occasions, in larger chains like the Starbuckses and Costas of this world, you'll connect to the network in the normal manner; when you see a pop-up web window you'll have to accept some terms and conditions and then you'll be permitted to get online. Some providers like 'The Cloud' offer free or limited Internet access, but you'll need to sign up for an account when you log in.

Protect Your Mac
On A Public Network

A network wouldn't be a network unless multiple devices were involved. This can be great when accessing content across devices on your own network, but in the public domain, you'll want to ensure your Mac's content is hidden from prying eyes. The easiest way to do this is to go to System Preferences > Sharing and make sure File Sharing does not have a tick box next to it.

Above: When using public networks, File Sharing should be turned off.

OTHER WAYS TO CONNECT TO THE INTERNET

While Wi-Fi networks and Ethernet are the two most likely ways you'll get online, there are alternative ways to connect your Mac to the Internet.

Below: A mobile hotspot can provide access to the internet when there's no Wi-Fi.

Mobile Broadband Dongles
And Wi-Fi Hotspots

If you plan on using your MacBook in a park or public space without Wi-Fi, you may consider a mobile device that uses the 4G LTE network to create a Wi-Fi hotspot your Mac can connect to in lieu of a stationary Wi-Fi connection. Available from many of the major mobile carriers, they can plug directly into your Mac or simply provide a wireless connection. You can buy pay-as-you-go Internet access or sign up to a monthly contract. When active, these devices will appear to you within the available Wi-Fi networks.

Tethering From Your Smartphone

Did you know your bundled smartphone data can be used as a mobile hotspot? This can sometimes be used to get online when there is no access to wired/Wi-Fi Internet, when you're in the park or at the beach.

Above: Wi-Fi hotspot on a phone.

Depending on your phone and provider, you can switch on the Wi-Fi hotspot functionality and piggyback on the 3G/4G connections. Some networks will make you buy an additional data bundle to enable Internet tethering, while others offer the bundle for free. Once the hotspot is set up and enabled, you'll be able to access the network in the usual way.

SHARING FILES AND INTERNET CONNECTIONS

Did you know you can share your Mac's Internet connection with other poor Internet-less souls and create a network of your own to share files with other Macs?

CREATING A WI-FI HOTSPOT FROM YOUR WIRED MAC

Now the circumstances in which you'll use this feature may be quite rare, but it's handy nonetheless. For example, if your Mac is connected to a wired modem and there's no Wi-Fi available, you can make that connection available to other devices. Essentially, it turns your Mac into a wireless router.

Step 5: Tick the Internet Sharing box and then click Start.

1. Head to System Preferences > Sharing.

2. Ensure 'Ethernet' is selected from the 'Share your connection from' menu.

3. Select Wi-Fi from the 'to computers using' section.

4. Select Internet Options (Wi-Fi Options in Mavericks) from the bottom right of the screen. Here, you'll be able to choose a name and set a password for your network. Hit OK.

5. From the left side of the screen tick the Internet Sharing box and select Start.

6. Now other devices will be able to connect to your network using the password you provide them with.

7. Internet Sharing can be turned off at any time by unticking the box within the Sharing portion of system preferences.

Above: It's easy to set up a computer to computer network to aid file transfers.

SHARING FILES OVER THE NETWORK

If you're using several computers over one network, or wish to share files with colleagues on the network, you can configure your Mac to make files available publicly over the Internet connection. Firstly, you need to head to System Preferences > Sharing and enable File Sharing by ticking the box in the sidebar.

Hot Tip

If you only wish to share certain files, create a folder on your desktop, place the files you wish to share in it and make that a shared folder by selecting it, tapping the shortcut Control + I and hitting the Shared Folder tick box.

Above: Enable File Sharing to allow other users to view certain folders.

Above: You can share your screen with other users and allow them to control it remotely.

This enables Mac and Windows users to view pre-determined files and folders on your network. To add which folders you wish to share, you can click the +/– buttons next to shared folders. While those settings are enabled, these files can be accessed by other users.

Accessing Shared Files On Other Computers

Just as you're able to make your files available to be shared on public networks, you can also browse to files on other Windows or Mac computers that have been made publicly available. If these computers are on the same network, you'll see them represented within the Shared sidebar in the Finder window. You can browse and open these files as you would when browsing your own computer.

Sharing Screens

Did you know it's possible to share your screen with other computers on the network? To share your screen is to allow others to see what you're working on and for them to remotely control apps and documents on your screen with their computer.

1. To allow access to your screen, head to System Preferences > Sharing and tick the Screen Sharing box in the sidebar.

2. In the Allow Access section you can allow anyone with a user account on your computer to take control, or select which users you'd like to have access.

3. To set up permissions, click the Computer Settings button. Here you can ensure users have to ask permission to access the screen (you'll get a notification you'll need to accept), or you can set up a password.

4. If other users are on a Mac, they'll see your screen in the Shared Devices area in Finder. Likewise, you'll find access to shared screens in your own Finder window.

Borrowing Another Computer's Optical Disc Drive

As we've already mentioned, some Mac models have dispensed with the CD/DVD drive to save space. If you really need to play a DVD, burn a CD or install disc-based software on your Mac,

Above: If your own Mac does not have an optical drive, it is possible to share the drive of another Mac on the network.

you can borrow another machine's drive rather than buying a USB Superdrive (*see* page 27). Before you begin, you need to check both computers are on the same network.

1. If you're sharing another Mac drive, head to System Preferences > Sharing on that Mac and tick CD/DVD sharing. You can choose whether permission is needed.

2. On the Mac that's doing the sharing, you should see a Remote Disc show up in the Finder window.

3. Browse to Remote Disc and double click the icon for the first Mac. If you chose to request permission, you can request it and then click on Accept on the other device.

4. Now you can use a disc as if it were inside your own computer.

Borrowing A Windows PC's Optical Drive

If a PC is set up to share its disc drive, you can access that on your Mac too:

1. On Windows 10, select the Control Panel and choose Hardware and Sound.

2. Choose 'DVD or CD sharing options' and select the check box for sharing.

3. The PC user can choose 'Ask me before allowing others to use my DVD drive' to ensure protection.

4. From here you'll see the Remote Disc option in the Finder window on the Mac borrowing the drive.

AIRDROP

AirDrop is another one of those handy Apple-only features and is probably the easiest way for Mac, iPhone and iPad owners to share content with each other. In this case, the Apple devices don't need to be on the same Wi-Fi network. As well as sharing files with each other, this can be handy for exchanging files between your own Apple devices, if you have more than one.

Above: AirDrop is an easy way to share content between Macs, other Macs and iOS devices.

Sharing Files With AirDrop

There are a few ways to share files, folders, text and so on using AirDrop. You'll find it within the Finder sidebar under Favorites or can access it by selecting Finder > Go > AirDrop. Whichever you choose, the Finder window will now search for other macOS and iOS devices running AirDrop in the vicinity.

> **Hot Tip**
>
> Files can also be shared with AirDrop by selecting them in a Finder window and selecting AirDrop from the Share button menu.

Once the Macs are showing within the Finder window, you can drag and drop any files you wish on to that user's profile picture, then press Send to process the request. Once the other user has accepted, the transfer will begin.

Receiving Files Via AirDrop

In order to receive files via AirDrop you will need to accept them. You will see a notification in the top right corner. Accepted files will begin transferring and will appear in the downloads folder when complete.

Step 2: The Mac will search for other devices which are in range.

Step 4: Select the device to connect to and then click Pair.

Step 4: Before a device is finally paired, the recipient will have to accept.

B IS FOR BLUETOOTH

With all of these fancy means of sharing over Wi-Fi using AirDrop, AirPlay and more, poor old Bluetooth has taken a back seat in recent years. However, the short-range connectivity tech is still built into all Macs, PCs and most mobile devices. It's handy for pairing peripherals like keyboards, mice and printers, and exchanging files over short distances.

Pairing Up Devices Via Bluetooth

First of all, ensure the device you want to pair with is switched on and has Bluetooth switched on and in discoverable mode. Without that you might as well not bother.

1. Turn on Bluetooth on your Mac by selecting the B icon in the menu bar.

2. Open Bluetooth preferences and your Mac will search for the discoverable devices that are in range.

3. You may see other keyboards, phones, tablets, speakers, printers and other devices depending on your location and set-up.

4. Select the device and click Pair. The Mac will examine the device and find the best way to communicate with it. Usually it will send users a keycode to type in or accept.

5. If applicable, you'll be able to hover over the paired device within the Bluetooth devices list in the menu bar and share files. Otherwise, head to Utilities, select Bluetooth File Exchange, choose a file from the Finder, choose the device and hit Send.

Pairing A Wireless Keyboard And Trackpad

We dealt with this briefly during set-up in Chapter Two, for wireless peripherals that were pre-paired with your Mac. If you want to buy and pair new ones, it's easily done.

1. Turn on the keyboard/trackpad via the button at the side.

2. Browse to System Preferences and select Keyboard/Trackpad, then Set Up Bluetooth Keyboard/Trackpad.

3. It'll take a couple of seconds to discover the keyboard. Once it appears, hit Continue.

Step 2: Select Set Up Bluetooth Keyboard/Trackpad.

4. If it's a keyboard you'll need to enter an eight-digit passcode. In the case of a trackpad it should automatically pair.

Sending Audio To Bluetooth Speakers

Bluetooth speakers are still quite popular and are certainly more abundant than those with AirPlay functionality (see page 170). To pair with Bluetooth speakers, follow the steps above. Then select System Preferences > Sound and select the speaker as the Output Device. This will ensure all audio is played through the external speakers.

Above: Bluetooth speakers can be set as the Output Device.

SHARING MEDIA FILES AND STREAMING CONTENT

Now all of the geeky networking stuff is out of the way, we can get on to some more enjoyable tasks, like beaming music, video and your screen to other devices via AirPlay.

Above: Click the AirPlay logo within iTunes to see the various options.

AIRPLAY

The Apple-to-Apple streaming technology is one of those neat tricks the company pulls to keep you within its ecosystem and using its gadgets. An AirPlay-enabled home, complete with like-minded devices, can revolutionize how you experience entertainment content. Over Wi-Fi you can beam content to the TV or a pair of speakers from your Mac and iOS devices.

APPLE TV

The Apple TV is a neat, fairly inexpensive (£149/$149) device resembling a hockey puck that plugs into your HD TV via the HDMI port. It enables you to rent movies and TV shows over the Internet and is also capable of streaming live and on-demand content from apps like Netflix, Sky News and the like. However, for our purposes it's most useful due to its ability to communicate wirelessly with your Mac and beam media to your television set.

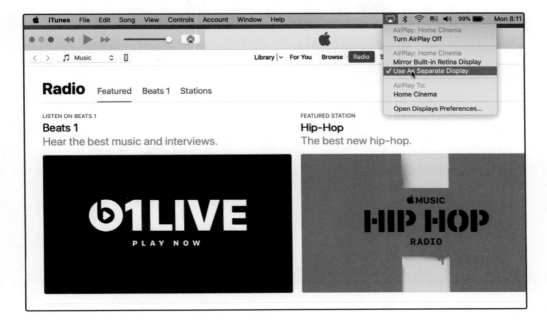

Above: Apple TV can communicate wirelessly with your Mac and beam media to the TV.

Streaming Music/Video With Apple TV

If you're on the same Wi-Fi or wired network as an AirPlay-enabled device like the Apple TV box, you're able to share iTunes media with that device.

Above: With Apple TV, media from iTunes can be played through the television.

Within iTunes, you'll see the AirPlay icon pictured. It takes two forms which you can see below. Click this icon and select Apple TV. Start playing your music or video in iTunes and within a few seconds you'll get audio and video coming through your television and its sound system. You can use the media controls on your Mac or the Apple TV remote to control playback.

AirPlay Mirroring

It's not just music and video you can send to an Apple TV box; if you want, you can send your whole screen wirelessly to your television using AirPlay Mirroring.

This allows you to view what you're doing on a larger screen (great if you're giving presentations or watching a video stream over the Internet), but also to extend your desktop to another screen so windows can be dragged on to the TV without plugging in an external cable. Here's how it's done.

1. To access AirPlay Mirroring, hit the AirPlay icon in the menu bar and select Apple TV under Connect to AirPlay Display.

2. This will turn the AirPlay icon blue and your desktop should now show up on your television.

3. Once you're connected, click the AirPlay icon again. Here you can select whether you want to 'Mirror Built in Display' or 'Us as a Separate Display'.

Hot Tip

Want to show off a photo slideshow on your TV? Use AirPlay Mirroring to connect to your TV. Open Photos, find the album of your choice and hit Play Slideshow.

Above: Apple built its own AirPlay enabled speaker with Siri controls. It's called HomePod.

4. This will automatically send audio to the Apple TV.

5. To turn off AirPlay Mirroring, click the blue AirPlay icon and hit Disconnect.

Other AirPlay-enabled Devices

If you want to stream music from your Mac (or iPhone, iPod touch or iPad for that matter) to a set of speakers, one option is to buy an AirPlay-enabled set of speakers. Apple now makes its own speaker called HomePod, which is designed specifically to work with Apple Music and has Siri controls. There are more on offer, and here are some of the most popular models.

- The B&W Zeppelin 2 or B&W Zeppelin Air (bowers-wilkins.com).

- Bose Soundlink Air Digital Music (Bose.com).

- Sonos One (Sonos.com).

- Libratone Zipp (libratone.com).

Hot Tip
Got some old speakers that you want to use to play music wirelessly? Connecting an AirPort Express to a pair of powered speakers makes them AirPlay compatible.

AirPlay 2

The newer version of AirPlay enables you to connect to multiple speakers at a time. This may be handy if you have a multiform audio system based upon AirPlay-enabled speakers like Apple HomePod. This way your music can spread through every room.

Connecting A Second Monitor

If you're not using an AirPlay-enabled display you can easily connect one using the requisite cables. That could mean using another computer on your desk to give you more screen space to work, or simply hooking up to the TV via HDMI to watch content on a bigger screen. Once you're connected, head to Displays in System Preferences to configure.

iTUNES HOME SHARING

iTunes Home Sharing is a pre-cursor to AirPlay, but remains very important. It makes all of your media files available across a Wi-Fi network. It allows you to access your Mac's entire iTunes media library on up to five different computers, iOS devices or an Apple TV device. In essence it's a great way to share your library without having to store the files on multiple devices.

Above: You can share your entire iTunes library with other devices on the same Wi-Fi network.

Setting Up iTunes Home Sharing

First of all, open iTunes and head to Preferences. Head to Sharing and select the tick box next to Share your home library on my local network. Here you can choose to share the entire library or just certain playlists. Once selected, those files will be available for playback within the devices listed above.

- **On other computers**: Open iTunes. The shared library will appear beneath the 'Shared' section of the sidebar.

- **On iOS devices**: Head to the Music/Video apps, select More > Shared.

- **On Apple TV**: Go to the Computers app where you'll see the shared iTunes library.

Above: The Mac's iTunes library shared to an iPhone.

PRINTING, SCANNING AND EXTERNAL DISPLAYS

Although the dominance of email has lessened the need for physical documents, a printer and scanner are still a necessity in some homes and offices. Here are some tips on adding more devices and displays to your network.

Above: Select the printer you have connected to your Mac.

CONNECTING A PRINTER TO YOUR MAC

Once, you had no choice but to tether your Mac physically to the printer via a component cable or USB. Now there are some other options, thanks to wireless technologies like Bluetooth and Wi-Fi.

USB Printers

If you're keeping your Mac on your desk, this might be the simplest and most reliable option. Connect your printer to the mains and turn it on. Connect the USB cable to both devices. It's likely that your Mac already contains the 'driver' software necessary to run it.

Wi-Fi-Enabled Printers And AirPrint

AirPrint allows you to print documents wirelessly over your Wi-Fi network from your Mac or iOS mobile devices.

Currently there are over 700 AirPrint-compatible printers available for your Mac from around 16 manufacturers. Apple keeps a list on its website (http://support.apple.com/kb/HT4356). Setup your printer using the instructions provided and connect to the Wi-Fi network.

Setting Up A Bluetooth Printer

We dealt with Bluetooth earlier in this section and you can pair up the device using the method shown on page 170.

Adding Printers To Your Network

Regardless of how you're hooking up your printers, you'll need to go to System

Above: Attempt to print a document: if no printer is listed, you will need to add one.

Preferences > Printers & Scanners to configure the device. Hit the + button to search for the printer. It should pop up in the list, allowing you to add it to the network. Alternatively, you can attempt to print a document (Command + P). If no printer is listed, hit Add Printer to find nearby or connectable printers.

Hot Tip

To share your printer with other Macs across the network, allowing other computers to use it, select the printer in System Preferences and tick 'Share this printer on the network'.

PRINTING ON MACS

In most document-creation and viewing apps on your Mac (the likes of Pages, Preview, Safari) you access the print settings in the File section of the menu bar or by hitting the shortcut Command + P.

Mastering The Print Settings

Before your document starts printing, you'll be asked to confirm a host of settings: layout, orientation, paper size, page range, number of copies, colour and paper choices. Select Show Details to configure the settings to your preference. Hit Print, and you're good to go.

Hot Tip

If you plan on burning an album or playlist to a CD in iTunes, you can easily print a case insert by hitting Command + P and selecting Print jewel case insert.

USING SCANNERS

'A scanner?' you ask. 'What is this? 1997? Who uses scanners?' Yes, we know, but wait until you have to print and sign an important document and get it back to the sender within the hour. Then you'll realize why this section is here.

Hooking Up A Scanner To Your Mac

A lot of modern printers have scanners built into them, so if you have one of these all-in-one multi-taskers, then you don't need to worry. If you have a standalone model, it's likely you'll hook it up via USB. Once it is connected, your Mac should recognize it and you're good to go.

Scanning In Documents

We haven't discussed it yet, but there's a dedicated app called Image Capture that's perfect for this business. Load it up and follow the steps.

1. Open the Image Capture app and place the document or photo face down on the scanning bed, so it's facing the glass surface.

2. Alternatively, if the scanner features a document feeder, you can feed it into the scanner.

3. Click Scan and Image Capture will automatically scan the document. You can choose whether you 'Detect Separate Items' in order to capture other aspects of the page.

4. Select 'Scan To' to save the scanned document to a location of your choosing.

		Name	Date	File Size	Aperture	Depth	Color Space
		IMG_0012.JPG	14 Oct 2012 12:17:35	3.5 MB	f/2.4	8	sRGB
		IMG_0013.JPG	14 Oct 2012 12:19:11	930.6 KB		8	sRGB
		IMG_0014.JPG	14 Oct 2012 12:23:17	2.5 MB	f/2.4	8	sRGB
		IMG_0015.JPG	14 Oct 2012 12:23:33	2.8 MB	f/2.4	8	sRGB
		IMG_0016.JPG	14 Oct 2012 12:39:28	2.7 MB	f/2.4	8	sRGB

Above: Image Capture is a dedicated app for scanning documents in to your Mac.

Hot Tip

To make corrections to the scanned document, open Preview and select Import From Scanner to open the file.

BACKING UP YOUR FILES

Somewhere around the turn of the century the excuse 'my hard drive failed' replaced 'the dog ate my homework'; only this time it was true! In this section we'll examine the plentiful tools available to Mac users to ensure they never lose work, media files or memories.

WHY BACK UP YOUR COMPUTER?

For every way there is to back up your data, there's a really good reason to do so. Before we delve into how to do it, here are just four reasons to ensure your data is safe at all times.

1. If you lose your Mac or it is stolen, your vital work documents are secured elsewhere in the iCloud or on hard drives ... that's if you backed up, of course.

2. If your Mac dies an untimely death, via accident or hardware failure, your photo and music collections do not have to die with it. They can easily be restored to a new machine ... if you took the time to back up.

Above: Recover mistakenly deleted files with Time Machine.

3. If you can't take your Mac with you everywhere, you can always access that office presentation, spreadsheet or your CV. That's if you backed up.

4. If you desperately need to return to an earlier time period, before you deleted your work files by accident, you can access it via your Time Machine. Only if you backed up, though.

Backing Up Using An External Hard Drive

Probably the easiest way to safeguard your files is to copy them over to an external hard drive, which can be transported around with you. External hard drives are relatively inexpensive with a massive 1 Terabyte USB hard drive costing around £50 ($70), right down to small USB memory sticks, which can be no more expensive than a couple of quid.

1.   In order to copy files from your Mac to a USB hard drive, simply plug it in to the USB port on your Mac.

2.   The disc image should appear on your desktop.

3.   Open the disc in a Finder window.

4.   Select and copy (Command + C) the files/folders you wish to back up and paste (Command + V) them within the new disc. Alternatively, drag and drop them.

Above: The external hard drive will appear in your Finder window.

5. Wait until the progress bar indicates that the file transfer is complete.

6. Be sure to hit the eject icon in Finder, or right click and select Eject to ensure the hard drive is ejected safely.

Hot Tip
For way, way faster file transfers, get yourself a Thunderbolt external hard drive, providing your Mac has a Thunderbolt port, that is.

Freeing Up Space With An External Hard Drive

Your Mac's hard drive can get really full, really quickly, especially if you have a large media collection. You can free up some space by moving files you don't access very often to an external hard drive for safekeeping.

1. To move files off your hard drive and on to an external hard drive, plug the drive in via the USB port and open it in a Finder window. Some new Macs don't have standard USB 3.0 ports anymore, so you may need a USB adaptor.

2. Select the files you wish to copy and move them onto the new hard drive as outlined previously.

3. Wait for the file transfer to complete and check they're sitting on the drive before ejecting the drive (*see left*).

4. Move all of the copied files on your Mac to Trash and empty to delete permanently.

Step 2: Select the files to be copied on to the hard drive, and drag them across to move them.

YOUR VERY OWN TIME MACHINE

For the smartest and most diligent back-up artists, Apple's Time Machine functionality is king. Not only does it back up the state of your entire Mac to an external hard drive, but it does so automatically on a scheduled basis and knows about all the changes you make. The idea is that you can revisit your Mac at a certain point in time and access lost, damaged or changed files. Even your favourite settings are saved.

Choosing A Hard Drive

You can use any compatible, dedicated USB hard drive to configure Time Machine. Providing there's enough space, it'll back up the contents of your Mac on a scheduled basis, providing it's plugged into your computer.

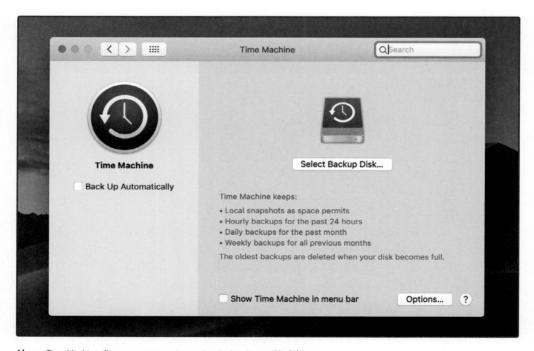

Above: Time Machine allows access to previous points in time in your Mac's history.

Setting Up Time Machine

First of all you'll need to open Time Machine in System Preferences and choose a disk drive for your backups.

1. Choose Select Backup Disk from the centre of the screen.

2. Select the external hard drive you have inserted into your Mac and select Use As Backup Disk. It is recommended you also tick the 'Encrypt Backup' box before doing so.

3. If you're using a physical hard drive it may ask you erase the content currently on the drive because of an incompatible file system. Be sure there's nothing important on the drive before you click Erase.

Hot Tip

If you have an AirPort Extreme base station, it supports USB hard drives. Plug this in and use it as you would a wireless Apple Time Capsule.

Step 1: Open the Time Machine app.

Step 2: Select the drive to save the back-up data to.

Step 3: Time Machine will now prepare to back up your Mac.

4. Once you've set up the Time Machine, the app will begin backing up your data. It will take a few hours to complete.

Scheduling Time Machine Back-ups

Provided your Time Machine is connected to your Mac, the Time Machine app will begin by backing up your data every hour. Over time it will store hourly back-ups for the last 24 hours, daily back-ups for the past month and weekly back-ups for all previous months. This means you'll be able to go back in time and access a version of your computer from any given week. Once the disc is full, the oldest versions will be deleted.

Above: Search through the stack of Finder windows to find old files.

Working With Time Machine

Now your Mac is backing itself up on the hour, every hour, you've got your very own DeLorean. Hit the Time Machine icon in the menu bar and select Enter Time Machine. This will whisk away all of your other windows and present you with a mountain of Finder windows stacked on top of each other. You can search within these Finder windows and move back and forth between them using the arrows at the foot of the screen to find your files. Once you've found the file, hit Restore and it'll be brought back to the present.

Time Machine Options

There are a couple of extra bits and bobs regarding Time Machine you should know about. These sit within

Above: To set up further preferences, click Options at the bottom right of the Time Machine app.

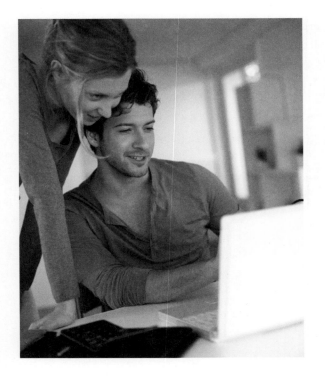

Options in the Time Machine. If you hit the tick box 'Back up when running off battery' it may take a bigger toll on battery life. Also, you can choose to be notified when older back-ups are deleted within this menu.

Hot Tip

Before you back up you'll be notified about the estimated size of the back-up. Make sure you have a hard drive large enough for the job.

BACKING UP WITH DISK UTILITY

Disk Utility will come in very handy later when we're troubleshooting, but it's also handy for backing up, burning and archiving some of the files on your Mac.

Above: Disk Utility is great for archiving files on your Mac.

Create Disk Image

Another way to archive files on your Mac is to use the Disk Utility application to create what's known as a 'disc image'. This allows you to create a virtual second hard drive within your Mac, where material you don't use very often can be compressed and stored in order to save space, and encrypted to keep out prying eyes. These compressed folders can then be burned to discs, moved to different hard drives or sent to other Mac users.

1. Move all of the files you want to archive into a folder.

2. Open the Utilities folder and select Disk Utility.

3. Hit File > New Image > New From Folder and select your folder in Finder.

4. Choose a name for the folder, choose a destination to save it, and whether you wish to compress it.

Step 4: Choose a name for the folder and where to save it.

5. Choose the level of encryption and select a password. This will be needed to open the Disk Image in the future. Don't lose this password.

6. Once the image has been created, it is yours to do with as you will.

BURNING TO DISC

It's also possible to store your files on CD/DVD by burning them from your hard drive. provided you have access to an internal or external optical disc drive (*see* page 165).

1. Place the disc in the optical drive to load an open Finder window.

2. Simply drag and drop the files you want to store.

3. Hit the Burn icon when you're finished.

Alternatively, you can go through the Disk Instructions listed to the left, and then simply hit Burn when the image has been created.

Complete Back-ups

There are several third-party applications that allow you to back up absolutely everything on your Mac, if disaster strikes and you need to restore from scratch. Try Carbon Copy Cloner or Crashplan.

THE POWER OF THE CLOUD

More and more people are choosing to utilize the cloud as a way to store and back up their files on the Internet. Using services like iCloud and Dropbox, among others, makes it easy to automatically save files and access them on multiple devices.

APPLE iCLOUD

We've talked extensively about iCloud in the book so far. This online storage solution pops up in several of the applications we've discussed, like Pages, iTunes, Safari, Calendar, Photos, Maps and more. The service is now an integral part of the Mac experience and there are two major components: iCloud and iCloud Drive. Here's how to get the best out of them.

Above: iCloud works with files from various applications.

What Does iCloud Sync?

iCloud is not a traditional back-up service. It's not really about transferring files for access later, it's more about keeping your information up to date and making it available across your devices. It's something that, once set up, you won't really think about using. For example:

1. Photos imported into Photos can be automatically sent to Photo Streams. This doesn't even count towards your free 5 GB storage!

2.   Calendar events created on your Mac are synced to your iOS devices.

3.   Music you've bought from iTunes will be instantly available to download on other devices with iCloud.

Signing Into iCloud

In all likelihood, you're already using iCloud and signed in or signed up when we set up your Mac in Chapter Two. If you're not, you can sign in at System Preferences > iCloud, using your Apple ID. From this menu you can also choose which apps you'd like to play nicely with iCloud.

Above: iCloud allows you to access your data across all your different devices.

Free iCloud Storage

Anyone with an Apple ID gets 5 GB of free iCloud storage with their device, which can be enough for some users. Look at it this way, iCloud doesn't physically store your music, movie and app purchases or photos, it just remembers which ones you've bought and allows you to access them elsewhere.

iCloud Drive

iCloud Drive is a cloud storage locker where you can save all the files and folders you need, for access across multiple devices, with syncing in real time. If you're working on a document saved in iCloud Drive, any changes you make will automatically be saved across all of the devices. This makes it ideal for storing documents.

Hot Tip

iCloud is useful for syncing data across devices, and if you go to iTunes > Preferences > Store and select Automatic downloads, music and apps your purchases will automatically be downloaded to your Mac.

Above: You can have your purchased items automatically downloaded.

Above: Selecting the information backed up to iCloud helps you manage your storage.

Here's how to enable the feature:

1. Enter System Preferences and select iCloud. Ensure the iCloud Drive box is ticked.

2. Click Options. Here you'll see a list of apps that store documents and data.

3. Here you can select Desktops and Documents folder, files from the Preview app, as well as Apple's iWork apps (Pages, Keynote, Numbers). Those documents you select will be automatically backed up to iCloud Drive.

iCloud Storage Options

The main reason you'll need more storage is if a large proportion of your storage is taken up by backing up entire iOS devices like iPads and iPhones, or you're storing a large selection of documents and your entire Photos Library from your Mac. To purchase more storage enter System Preferences > iCloud > Manage > Buy More Storage. This will be charged to your Apple ID credit card info.

Storage options:

50 GB
£0.79/$0.99
per month

200 GB
£2.49/$2.99
per month

2 TB
£6.99/$9.99
per month
(can be shared with
family members)

Left: There are three options
for how much extra storage
to buy.

Using iCloud Drive

Once you're backing up documents on iCloud Drive you'll be able to access them from a special iCloud section of the Finder window. Here you can select and use the documents as you normally would, knowing that changes will also be reflected in iCloud.

OTHER CLOUD BACK-UP SERVICES

Aside from iCloud, there are loads of ways to back up your data online and prevent the disaster of lost files and memories. They all offer some degree of free storage and allow you to save and sync documents straight to folders stored on your Mac, making them available everywhere.

Dropbox

Dropbox is one of the current leaders in the marketplace. It offers multi-platform support (Android, iOS, Mac, PC) and offers 2 GB of free storage.

Above: Microsoft OneDrive is a popular method of backing up files and sharing them with other devices.

Google Drive

If you use Google Mail and Google Docs, then Google Drive might be the storage solution for you. It gives you a whopping 15 GB of free storage (spread across your Google Accounts).

Microsoft OneDrive

If you're a Microsoft loyalist (Hotmail, Outlook, etc.) and have a PC at home too, you may wish to try SkyDrive. It comes with 5 GB of storage, but some long-time users may be able to get 25 GB through promotions.

KEEPING YOUR MAC SECURE

There's more to protecting your Mac than backing up files. You'll need to be prepared to secure your online privacy, keep tabs on your passwords and keep your children safe online.

IS MALWARE AN ISSUE?

One of the main reasons people choose Macs is their perceived invulnerability to the external security threats that tend to strike down Windows PCs. Generally speaking, you've much less to worry about. There are no known instances of the traditional viruses, but one or two adware/malware threats are slowly creeping in as the popularity of Macs rises. In terms of security threats, you're less susceptible to adware and malware, but there are still plenty of tools to shore up your defences. For extra peace of mind, you may wish to install some security software.

Security Updates

Every now and then you'll get a Software Update notification promising only a Security Update. Ensure you download and install these at the earliest possible opportunity. They'll nullify any threats or vulnerabilities Apple may have discovered.

Hot Tip

In Security and Privacy in System Preferences, you can choose from where you allow apps to be downloaded. We suggest you choose the setting that specifies the Mac App Store and identified developers.

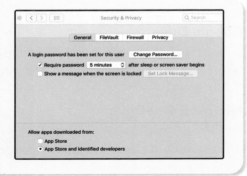

Apps

As we mentioned, the Mac App Store automatically vets all of the applications, but if you download from the Internet, Apple uses a tool called Gatekeeper to ensure these apps have not been tampered with and are not produced by known developers of malicious software. It will block these apps from being installed. If infected apps are uncovered, Apple's Sandboxing tool stops them messing with other apps and data.

PASSWORDS

Ah, the password. The guardian of everything we hold dear in our digital world. You've probably got loads of them, and if you haven't you probably should have. Here's how they can help you keep your Mac secure.

Above: Your system password is required to change computer settings.

System And Administrator Passwords

When we set up the Mac, we created a password. Not only does this let you log in, but is also the administrator password, required when you want to make changes to your computer's settings; for example, by clicking the padlocks in System Preferences windows. You can also make other users administrators.

Use iCloud Keychain To Store Your Passwords

If you're wondering how you're going to remember all of those long passwords for all of those apps, websites, accounts and more, you don't have to. iCloud Keychain will manage that for you. It stores your passwords and credit card information safely and syncs it across other devices. It'll also help you create complex passwords for Safari, which you also don't have to remember.

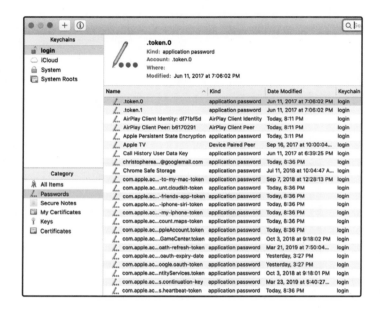

Left: Keychain Access can help you recover forgotten passwords.

Enable iCloud Keychain

Head to System Preferences > iCloud and tick iCloud Keychain. You may be asked to enter an Apple ID password here. You will also need to set up a 6-digit code that will allow the keychain information to be synced to other devices.

Accessing The Keychain

iCloud Keychain information is housed in its specific applications. For example, if you've forgotten a password you use for a website, you can find it in Safari. Go to Safari > Preferences > Passwords and use your computer's password to reveal them.

Locking Your Screen

If you're using a Mac at home or at work, chances are you'll need to leave it unattended from time to time, potentially leaving it open to prying eyes. You can fix this by locking the device after a period of inactivity without having to log out.

1. Go to System Preferences > Security and Privacy.

Hot Tip

If you actually feel like physically locking your MacBook as you would a pushbike or a door, then you can pick up some neat solutions online.

2. Click the lock and enter your administrator
    password to make changes.

3. Select Advanced and tick 'Log out after __ minutes
    of inactivity' and select the amount of time.

4. Alternatively, within Security and Privacy toggle the
    setting that requires a password to be entered a
    certain amount of time after the screen saver kicks in.

Once the screen is locked, it has the same effect as
shutting the lid on your Mac or putting it to sleep.
You'll need to enter the password to return to work.

Step 3: Select after how many minutes of inactivity
the computer will automatically log out.

Notifications On The Lock Screen

Lock screen notifications, alerting you to emails
and incoming messages can be handy, but you don't
necessarily want everyone to see them, especially if
it's a preview of a sensitive email. You can disable
lock screen notifications for each app by heading to
System Preferences > Notifications and unticking the
'Show in lock screen' box for each app. A less extreme
solution is just to turn off previews. You'll know you
have a notification, but no one will see the contents.

Above: Deselect Show notifications on lock screen.

Logging Out

If you're on a Mac that has multiple users it's advisable to log out of your account at the end
of your session. Make sure everything you're working on is saved and hit the Apple logo in the
menu bar, then just click Log Out. This will take you to the lock screen and will require a
password from the next user to log back in.

ACCOUNTS

Sharing is caring, and we're happy to let other people use our Mac, but that doesn't mean we want all of our files and documents exposed. That's why it's wise to set up a guest account, or accounts for each member of the family.

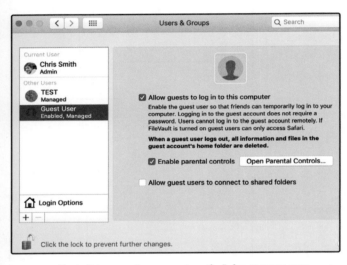

Above: Set up a guest user account specifically for a temporary user.

Hot Tip

It's always worth having a guest account active. If a thief gets hold of your Mac, and logs into the guest account, then the Find My Mac (*see* page 204) portion of iCloud can track the location.

Guest Accounts

These are handy on the rare occasions someone needs to use your Mac. Head to System Preferences > Users and Groups, hit Login options and tick Allow guests to log into this computer. You'll need to be logged in as an administrator as well. They won't have access to anything you don't wish to share and won't need a password to log in.

New User Account

If other people use your Mac regularly, it's worth giving them their own account. Here they can have access to all apps, their own settings and private document storage. More importantly, they won't be messing with yours. Effectively it creates an entirely new Mac. To set up a new account:

1. Go to Users and Groups in System Preferences.

2. Click the lock in the bottom left and enter the administrator's password.

3. Click the + icon to add a new account.

4. In the pop-up window add the name, password and choose the type of account for the user: Administrator (everything that you can do, they can do), Standard (no tinkering with other accounts), Managed with Parental Controls (good to keep the kids on the straight and narrow).

Step 4: Set up the various account details, such as name and password.

5. Click Create, click the thumbnail to choose a profile pic and, if they have one, enter their Apple ID.

Quickly Switching Between Accounts

Anyone with an account can log in on start up, but it's also easy to Quick Switch accounts by hitting the name section of the menu bar, clicking another account and entering the password. None of the current user's apps or data is lost.

Above: To switch accounts, click on the user name on the menu bar, and select another user.

Right: If Find My Mac is ticked, proceed to iCloud.com to track down your stolen computer.

LOST OR STOLEN MACS

We hope this never happens to you, but if you lose your Mac or some light-fingered so-and-so steals it, there's still a chance for redemption with Find My Mac. Otherwise, if you've backed up your data you can reinstall your old Mac on to a new one.

Using Find My Mac

Firstly, go to System Preferences > iCloud and ensure Find My Mac is ticked. Then head to iCloud.com within your browser and log in using your details. You'll see 'Find iPhone' but your Mac is also here.

If the Mac is in use, you'll see its exact GPS position on a map. Your next step is to call the police and have them help you to recover your property. Vigilantism is not encouraged.

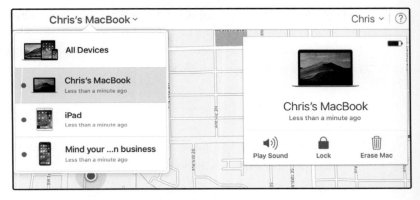

Above: If the stolen Mac is in use, its location can be tracked by GPS and will be displayed on a map.

Finding, Locking And Remote Wiping Your Mac

If you've just left your Mac under the sofa cushions you can use Find My Mac to make it play a sound. However, if you think there's no way you're getting your Mac back, you can choose to lock it or even remotely wipe all of the information using Find My Mac. Log in at iCloud.com, select Find iPhone and identify the device on the map. Click the 'i' icon and select Lock or Erase.

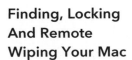

MacBook Airs are small enough that you can lose them around the house. Within Find My Mac, identify the device, select Play Sound and you should be able to hone in on the alert that sounds.

Above: Through Find My Mac the stolen Mac can be locked or wiped.

MIGRATION ASSISTANT

We discussed this when setting up in Chapter Two. It's a way to move all of your information from an existing Mac or an existing back-up to a new Mac. In this case, as our Mac is lost, stolen or broken, we're moving data from a back-up, so follow these instructions.

1. Firstly, connect the drive to your new Mac either physically or on the same wireless network.

2. Head to Applications > Utilities > Migration Assistant. You'll need to enter your administrator password. This will close down all apps.

3. When Migration Assistant loads, choose the option to move data 'from a Mac, Time Machine backup, or startup disk'.

4. Choose the drive you want to copy from. If it's a Time Machine disk you'll need to enter the password.

5. Choose the back-up you want to restore from, and select everything you want to transfer (apps, user accounts and more).

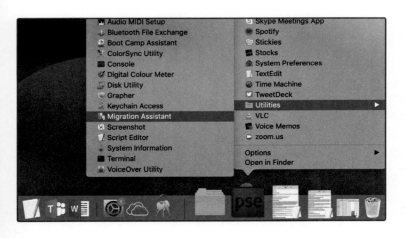

6. Hit Continue to begin the transition. It may take a while, but when you're done you'll have a new Mac exactly how you left it before the old one was lost, stolen or broken.

Step 2: Choose Migration Assistant from the Utilities window.

FILEVAULT, FIREWALL, PRIVACY AND PARENTAL CONTROLS

Your Mac has a huge array of security tools at its disposal beyond the data back-ups and the humble password. Here are some further features the more security and safety conscious among you may wish to deploy.

WHAT IS FILEVAULT AND WHEN DO YOU USE IT?

If having multiple user accounts, iron-clad passwords and a screen that locks the instant you step away isn't quite enough security to give you peace of mind, you should deploy FileVault. It ensures that even if someone does get their hands on your files, then they cannot decrypt that data without a password.

Turning On And Using FileVault

Encrypting your hard drive isn't a step that should be taken lightly. FileVault scrambles everything, only making it viewable to those with login passwords. Should you lose the password and a specially generated recovery key, it's difficult to get access to your data. Only those housing very confidential data should deploy it. If happy to proceed, take the following steps.

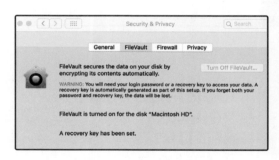

Above: FileVault will give you added security, but it's best to use it only if your data is very sensitive.

1. Navigate to System Preferences > Security and Privacy > FileVault.
2. Turn On FileVault.
3. Add the list of user accounts you wish to be able to log in once encryption is complete.
4. Make a copy of the recovery key and store it somewhere safe.
5. When complete, click Continue and then restart your Mac.

PUTTING UP A FIREWALL

The Firewall protects you from unwanted incoming Internet traffic. What this means is that nothing can connect to your computer unless you want it to. It's advised that you turn Firewall on in Security and Privacy.

Above: Choose which incoming connections to block.

To Block Or Not To Block

By clicking the Firewall Options button, you can modify which incoming connections to select. You can block all incoming connections that aren't for 'basic Internet services' and even go into 'stealth mode' that will hide your Mac completely from unwanted communications.

CONFIGURING PRIVACY SETTINGS

The Privacy section of System Preferences deals with the applications you have installed on your computer and what exactly those apps are allowed to access.

Right: Choose exactly what certain apps have access to.

Above: Turn off location services to keep your whereabouts hidden.

What Can Access What?

When other applications request permission to access apps like Calendar, Contacts and Reminders that information will appear here. You can revoke these permissions at any time in the Privacy section.

Above: Set up various preferences for what children can access.

Location Services

As we discussed earlier in Chapter Two when setting up your Mac, location services can be great when searching the Internet and using the Maps app, but if you wish to conceal your Mac's location, you can untick location services in System Preferences > Privacy. This will also prevent any other apps accessing your location.

Above: Revoke permission for certain apps to access other apps.

Parental Controls

If you've got kids and they're using your Mac then you may wish to limit the time they're able to use the computer, what they can access online, which apps they're allowed to use, whom they're allowed to contact and more.

Enabling Parental Controls

Firstly, you'll need to create a user account for your young ones (unless you want those controls to apply to you, of course!). Head to Parental Controls in System Preferences and click on that user account (you may need to enter your administrator password to make changes) and then hit Enable parental controls. You can now configure the following settings.

- **Apps**: Add or subtract which applications that user is allowed to access.

- **Web**: Restrict access to the Internet, giving access to only the websites you want them to see.

- **Stores**: Prevent your youngster from going on an iTunes spending spree, while also limiting access to age-restricted content.

- **Time Limits**: Set up weekend and weekday time allowances, while setting up a 'bedtime' to ensure they're not up all night.

Above: Restrict access to any unsuitable websites.

- **Privacy**: Here you can keep apps from requesting access to apps like Contacts, Reminders, Calendar and more.

- **Other**: Here you can restrict assess to the Mac's built-in camera, stop them changing the password and even hide swear words in the dictionary.

- Click the lock again to save these changes.

Above: Other options include hiding profanities in the dictionary.

GENERAL ONLINE SECURITY TIPS

During this chapter we've furnished you with everything you need to know about keeping your Mac secure, but we'd feel better if you also have these next few tips about staying safe online at your disposal.

○ **Remember to log out**: It can be a pain, but when you've finished using email and social-network accounts online (especially on a PC used by others) remember to log out of your accounts.

Above: AutoFill can save time but use with care.

○ **AutoFill**: This setting in Safari and other web browsers saves you from filling in web forms by automatically filling things like your name, address, username, password and credit card numbers. It's very useful, but be mindful of who has access to your web browser if you're using it.

○ **Hacked**: If for any reason you feel the security of any of your online accounts has been compromised – this includes your iTunes/iCloud/Apple ID password – then change it immediately. Clues that you might have been hacked can be your friends receiving spam messages or emails or posts to Facebook or Twitter you don't recognize.

○ **Tracked**: Most browsers now have a Do Not Track request mode, which stops advertisers following you around the Internet. In Safari, this lives in Preferences > Privacy.

Right: Stop advertisers from tracking you via the Internet.

MY MAC IS RUNNING SLOW

There are many and varied reasons for your Mac having performance issues. If you start seeing that spinning beach ball and programs are slow to react, it may be time to take action.

Above: Find out what is taking up space on the hard drive.

FREEING UP HARD-DRIVE SPACE

After a particularly filling Sunday roast, we all slow down a little bit and it's the same with your computer when the hard drive has too much stuff on it. A full hard drive slows performance. Ideally, your hard drive shouldn't be more than 90 per cent full.

Above: The Mac HD Info screen displays available space.

Above: The bottom of the Finder window will show how much space is free.

Checking Your Hard-drive Space

The easiest way to see how much space you have available is to select the Apple logo from the menu bar. Choose About This Mac and then select Storage. That'll tell you what's taking up the majority of your space. Hit Manage to see exactly which apps are commandeering the space. The bottom of the Finder window will also tell you how much you have available.

Moving Before Deleting

Just because you're removing items from your Mac, it doesn't mean you need to delete them. As we explained in the previous chapter, you can move any files you don't want to an external hard drive before deleting them.

How To Delete Stuff

Once you've safely deposited any important files elsewhere, you can set about getting some of that space back. Simply identify the apps, files and folders you want to delete and drag them into Trash. When you're done, you can empty the Trash by right clicking and

Above: Right click on files and select Move to Trash to delete.

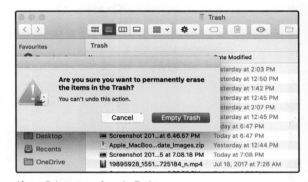

Above: Deleting items from the Trash is permanent.

The easiest way to delete apps and games you don't use is to click the Launchpad. Hold down the mouse or trackpad buttons and they'll start jiggling. Hit the 'X' icons to get rid of them.

Above: When the icons start jiggling, click the X to delete.

Hot Tip

If you can't see what's taking up all that space on your hard drive, download a piece of software called DiskInventoryX. It'll index your hard drive and you'll be able to see what's what.

selecting Empty Trash. Only then will the files be gone from your computer. Warning: once they're gone, they're gone for good.

PhotoScape X (Macintosh HD/Applications)
Application, 159.1 MB

What To Delete?

Unused apps and games can take up a lot of space and media files like photos, videos and movies can often be a killer. Moving them off your hard drive can save the most space.

Left: DiskInventoryX is a piece of software which will detail how much space is being used and by what.

Hot Tip

Wondering why your Mail folder is taking up so much space? Well, it's all those attachments in your inbox. Hit Mail > Preferences > Accounts > Account Information and change the Download Attachments setting to 'Never'.

MEMORY

Memory overload is probably the number one cause of slow performance. As we discussed in Chapter One, the RAM in your Mac allows you to keep everything running, but when it gets too much, your computer's efficiency takes a hit.

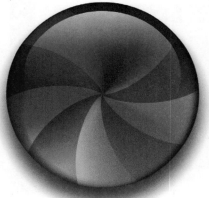

The Beach Ball And Other Signs Of Memory Overload

If you see the little spinning beach ball pop up on screen when you try to do something, that's your computer's memory trying to summon the power to perform the task. Other signs of memory overload include crashing apps, higher temperatures, a loud fan and the keyboard being slow to react.

How To Check On Your Memory

You can take a look at how well your memory is holding up by opening the Activity Monitor in Utilities and selecting Memory. This will show you a Memory Pressure graphic. The more strain on the memory, the higher the pressure. If the graph shows red, the memory is under duress. In the list above you can also view which apps are taking up the most memory.

Above: If the Memory Pressure graph in the Activity Monitor is red, there is too much strain.

Reducing The Strain

The easiest way to get your computer running at full speed again is simply to quit the apps you're not using. Do this while Activity Monitor is open and you'll see the stress lessen immediately on the pressure monitor. Quitting the apps will also help preserve your battery life. To batch-quit applications hit

Above: Hold down Command + Option + Escape to access the Force Quit menu and quit any applications causing problems.

Command + Option + Escape and Force Quit the apps in the list.

High-powered Tasks

Sometimes the strain on the memory isn't due to multiple apps, but one power-hungry application. When editing hi-res photos or editing hi-def video, you need lots of memory, otherwise everything will be done at a snail's pace.

Can I Get More Memory?

In Chapter One we discussed buying and configuring your Mac with sufficient memory. It used to be quite simple to do, but with newer models it's become nigh-on impossible for untrained people and definitely inadvisable to do it by yourself. For a start you will void your warranty.

Hot Tip
You can quickly see which apps are using significant amounts of memory by clicking the battery icon in the memory bar.

THE CPU

Your computer's processor has a heavy workload, and when it becomes a little too stressed this can also slow down your Mac. Your CPU (Computer Processing Unit) is the something that can't be replaced, but like memory there are simple ways to reduce the load.

How To Gauge CPU Usage

In Activity Monitor, click the CPU tab and you'll see which programs are taking up the highest percentage of the CPU's workload. At the foot of the window you'll also see the Active and Idle percentages. In an ideal world, the Idle percentage should be as high as possible, but if it drops below 50 per cent you could be taking a performance hit.

Helping Out The CPU

It's quite easy to give your CPU a more comfortable workload by easing up on the amount of apps it has to manage. Quit the ones you're not using, especially the ones demanding lots of power.

Process Name	% CPU	CPU Time	Threads	Idle Wake Ups	PID	User
coreservicesd	60.8	8:02.17	4	1	111	root
Disk Inventory X	22.3	2:15.46	5	0	63164	chrissmith
Activity Monitor	11.1	0.84	9	3	63247	chrissmith
kernel_task	9.4	22:27:09.38	148	471	0	root
launchservicesd	2.9	7:33.01	5	0	84	root
sysmond	1.9	50.38	5	0	48683	root
airportd	1.8	1:49:28.27	11	5	125	root
WindowServer	1.6	1:41:22.46	10	2	55365	_windowserver
locationd	1.1	29:09.51	6	2	89	_locationd
hidd	0.9	4:46:58.95	6	0	102	_hidd
iconservicesagent	0.5	27.24	4	0	60498	chrissmith
Preview	0.5	7:35.61	5	0	57643	chrissmith
thermald	0.5	51:49.94	3	0	205	root
bluetoothd	0.2	1:07:56.33	3	0	101	root
mds	0.2	43:23.73	8	2	72	root
routined	0.2	20.38	7	0	55507	chrissmith
mdworker_shared	0.1	0.10	4	0	63242	chrissmith
TextEdit	0.1	9:03.80	5	1	57154	chrissmith

Above: See how much of the CPU workload programs take up.

Hard-Drive Failure

A failing hard drive is the most worrying diagnostic for a slow Mac. If you're seeing that spinning beach ball when you try to open apps it could be a sign your storage device is on the blink. We'll talk more about disk maintenance on page 225.

> ## Hot Tip
> Is your desktop cluttered with loads of files? Clean it up. It can seriously slow down your computer.

CAN'T STAND THE HEAT

These MacBooks don't half get hot from time to time.

They shouldn't, but they do. Sometimes having them on your knee can get uncomfortable and even typing on them can be unpleasant. That's the last thing we want.

Curing A Hot MacBook

As we'll discuss frequently during this chapter, a good old-fashioned reset cures many of the ills you may be experiencing. Give your Mac a power cycle and see if this helps, and turn it off at night rather than putting it to sleep to give it a rest. If that doesn't help, you may need to perform what's known as an SMC reset (see page 222).

APP PROBLEMS AND THE GREAT RESET

In this section we'll deal with misbehaving apps and other anomalies within the macOS operating system, and how, more often than not, a simple restart can sort things out.

A RESTART CAN HELP ... MOSTLY

If you're experiencing problems with your Mac a simple restart can eliminate the problem. There are loads of problems a restart can fix, so let's dig in.

Forced Restart

This is far less common on newer versions of macOS. However, your Mac might just decide to restart spontaneously, or will display 'You need to restart your computer because of a ...' message. This is known as a Kernel Panic. There's nothing you can do in these circumstances but bite the bullet. If it happens once, don't worry too much. If it keeps happening, you may have bigger problems on your system.

Ways To Restart And Shut Down Your Mac

The Mac is teeming with ways to restart. Command + Control + power/eject button cuts straight to the chase; Apple logo > Restart or Control + power/eject brings up the shutdown options. The Mac will start straight back up again. Enter your login password and you should be good to go.

Above: The Restart dialogue box will ask you to confirm, or restart automatically if you do not respond within a given amount of time.

Left: One occasion on which you may wish to perform an SMC reset is if Bluetooth is not working correctly. Follow the steps below to do this.

The Grand SMC Reset

There's a reset and then there's a RESET. Sometimes when your Mac is experiencing problems an SMC (System Management Controller) reset can help. The SMC is responsible for the functionality of the power button, the system fan, which helps regulate temperature, the automatic screen and keyboard backlight brightness, battery performance, charging, sleep mode, trackpad controls and more. Here are some circumstances in which you may wish to perform an SMC reset.

- Poor **Bluetooth** performance.
- **Slow** performance.
- Mac not waking from **sleep** or failing to respond when you open the lid.
- **Power button** not responding.
- **Battery not charging**, taking too long to charge, not showing correct status.
- Fan running **loudly**/Mac running too hot.
- **USB devices** not showing when plugged in.

How To Perform An SMC

1. Shut your Mac down completely (Apple logo > Shut Down...).
2. Connect the power adapter.

3. On the keyboard, press Shift-Control-Option on the left side, then press the power button at the same time. Hold for 10 seconds.
4. Release them at the same time.
5. Press the power button to turn on the computer.

Note: There are different methods for desktop Macs and older MacBooks with removable batteries. Go to http://support.apple.com/kb/ht3964 for details.

The NVRAM Reset

If you're experiencing problems with your computer's audio performance, your Mac starts up from a different disc than the one you selected, or you see a question mark when you start up your Mac, you should perform a NVRAM reset (called PRAM on older Macs).
Here's how to do it.

1. Shut your Mac down.
2. Press the power button.
3. Hold Command, Option, P + R together. You may need to do this for 20 seconds.
4. You will hear a startup sound, ignore it and wait for the second startup sound.
5. Release the keys.

APP WOES

Apps are great, apps are fun, apps turn a Mac into the 'do everything' device we know and love, but they can't half be a pain in the rear end at times. Here's how to remedy the situation when they act up.

Apps Are Always Quitting On Me

Every now and again, you'll notice that all of a sudden an app you're using will crash without warning. You'll get a pop-up informing you that the app quit unexpectedly. Like you didn't know this. Here are a few tips for misbehaving apps.

Frozen Apps

If you're using a Mac with a slower CPU and less RAM, you'll be used to apps freezing on you and that spinning beach ball replacing your cursor. There are two things you can do: wait or quit. It may come around and if you're working on an unsaved item, we'd recommend a little patience. If the app is still unresponsive and doesn't even abide to the regular Command + Q notice to quit, you can Force Quit the app (Command + Alt + Escape).

Tips For Mischief-making Apps

1. Make sure you're running the most recent version of the app. If not, update it online or through the App Store by clicking Updates.

2. Consider ditching the app completely. Quite often the problem isn't something you can solve; apps have bugs that cause them to crash and freeze. Try an alternative or search the web for known issues.

3. Does the app always crash/freeze when you try to open a particular document? It could be the fault of the file rather than of the app.

4. Perform a system restart; this often irons out wrinkles in apps.

5. Check your disc space and your memory. All of these factors can contribute to app failure.

6. As we mentioned earlier, a hard drive on the blink could be causing problems (*see page 220*).

No updates available.

Good news, you're running the latest version of Skype.

OK

Hot Tip

You can check you're running the most up-to-date version of the software by searching and checking for updates in the menu bar of most apps.

BIGGER PROBLEMS: WHEN A RESTART ISN'T THE SOLUTION

If we've said it once, we've said it a thousand times; a restart solves most of life's (a Mac's) problems, but what about when it doesn't? What about when you can't access apps or open your files without the spinning beach ball popping up? What if your Mac keeps randomly restarting or the display isn't working? It's time to check that hard drive.

USING DISK UTILITY

The first port of call in these situations is the Disk Utility app, which, unsurprisingly, lives in your Utilities folder. We touched upon it briefly when discussing backing up our files. Here we'll be using it for a little first aid.

Opening The First Aid Box

Think your hard drive may be on the way out? The apps slowing to a crawl? You're hearing weird noises and it's heating up? You can check on the health of the hard drive by hitting First Aid from the Disk Utility app in utilities. Once complete, the First Aid check will let you know if there are any problems and then seek to repair them.

Above: Running a First Aid check on your Mac can diagnose and repair issues.

Verifying And Repairing The Disk

Think your hard drive may be on the way out? You hear that whirring noise, apps won't open and the fan is blowing a gale? You can check the health of the hard drive by selecting

Verify Disk. If all is good, you'll see a green message saying 'The Volume Macintosh HD appears to be ok'.

If the live verification reveals issues, you need to take further steps. You can attempt to Repair the disk.

- **If you have a macOS installation disc**: Insert the disc, restart the computer, hold down the C key and then choose your language and select Disk Utility > Repair Disk.

- **On a Mac with no physical installation disc**: Restart the Mac, press Command + R to bring up the Utilities options and select Disk Utility > Repair Disk. You'll notice there are various options to perform a clean install of macOS and restore your Mac from a Time Machine back-up. We'll get to those shortly.

MY MAC WON'T START

Problems with your Mac can result in the device failing at start-up, leaving you unable to log in and access your files. A blue screen, a grey screen or a flashing question mark usually manifests in this case. Sometimes it won't start up at all. While this could mean a hardware or software failure, there are some steps you can take before calling in the tech heavies.

Steps To Get Your Mac Back On Track

Your first step is to check for the obvious. Is the Mac's battery dead? Is the screen brightness down? Once you've ruled that out, it's time to check the hard drive for problems.

- **Repair Disk**: If you can get this far, follow the instructions above to run a First Aid test on your Mac. Select Disk Utility > First Aid. If errors are found, the Mac will attempt to repair them.

DISPLAY PROBLEMS

Is your display appearing pixelated? Is it completely freaking out or has it stopped working completely? Don't panic! There are steps you can take to solve this before running to the Geniuses. Before we proceed ... are you sure the brightness is turned up?

Check For Software Updates

Hit the Apple logo and browse to Software Update. If there's an update to your operating system, or a graphics update, install it. This could resolve the issue.

Restarts

The first step in these situations is, naturally, to perform a normal restart. If you don't have any joy there, try the NVRAM and SMC resets outlined earlier in this chapter. There's a good chance this could return your display to health.

Safety First

Performing a Safe Boot can help when Macs refuse to start at all. It can also help when identifying screen issues. Booting in this way allows you to check if the issues persist. If they do, it's likely to be hardware-related.

Still No Joy?

If nothing in this section has solved your problem and the errors are still presenting themselves, it might be time to head to the Apple Store or call support. However, there is something else you can try first ...

A NEW START

You've taken all the steps you can to improve your Mac's performance, updated the apps, maxed out memory, run Disk Utility and repaired any errors, gone through all of the checks and you're still having problems. Sometimes the only way to fix the foundations is to knock the house down and rebuild.

OPTIONS FOR REINSTALLING YOUR MAC

There are several ways to go about wiping the slate clean: you can completely erase your hard drive; you can reinstall the operating system, while keeping all your files; or you can restore from a Time Machine back-up.

Clean Reinstall Of macOS

If there are a few niggling bugs in your system that you just can't shake, maybe a few corruptions here and there, you may wish to try a clean install of macOS. This shouldn't affect any of your files and settings on your Mac but it's wise to ensure all of your files are backed up just in case (see page 182)

- **Latest Version:** Restart the Mac and press Option + Command + R until a spinning globe appears and then release the keys. This will guide you to installing the latest version of macOS onto your computer. For our purposes, that's macOS Mojave v 10.14.

macOS Mojave

To set up the installation of macOS Mojave, click Continue.

Above: A clean reinstall may solve many issues.

- **Your computer's original version**: If you want to return to the version of macOS that came with your Mac, restart your Mac and upon restart Press and hold Shift + Option + Command + R until a spinning globe appears, then release the keys.

From this point, you'll need to follow the on-screen instructions to Reinstall macOS. Once complete you'll be able to begin using your Mac with the clean install.

Hot Tip

Once the install is complete head to Software Update to ensure you have all the most up-to-date features (for example macOS Mojave v 10.14 instead of the retail version).

Reinstall From Time Machine

Remember the Time Machine process we went through in Chapter Six? Here's another occasion when it can save the day. Restoring from a Time Machine back-up lets you go back in time to when your computer wasn't so stuttery.

Above: Reinstalling macOS can be a last resort when attempting to resolve troublesome issues.

1. Restart your Mac, ensuring the Time Machine back-up drive is connected.

2. Turn the power on and press Command + R.

3. From the Disk Utility menu, select Restore From Time Machine Backup.

4. Select the Drive and the back-up you wish to install from and you're good to go.

There are two points to be aware of here:

1. You should only restore from a Time Machine back-up that was made from that Mac; if you're looking to install the data on another Mac, use Migration Assistant (*see* page 206).

2. Be warned that any data you've saved after that back-up will be erased.

Dealing With Lost And Damaged Files

If you haven't backed up your files regularly and you've accidentally deleted a file or folder, the chances are it's gone for ever. But there are steps you can take to bring it back from the dead. There are several pieces of third-party software you can use to attempt a recovery. See the 100 Top Apps section for advice (*see* pages 252–53).

Revert To Previous Versions

Some Apple-made apps on your Mac automatically save versions of documents you're working on. So if you over-save a document by accident or a file becomes corrupted, you can return to a previous version. In the application

Above: There are various recovery apps which can be used to try to retrieve lost data.

select File > Revert To > Browse Old Versions. You'll see a Time Machine-style interface, where you can browse through all older versions and choose one to restore.

Above: Some apps on your Mac have a Time Machine-style function which allows you to access previous versions of the file.

DEALING WITH POOR BATTERY LIFE

While computing technology continues to accelerate year upon year, we've still not reached that utopia where your MacBook's battery life can last longer than a few hours without the mains.

STAYIN' ALIVE

MacBook battery life has dramatically improved in the last few years, to the point that it can get you through an entire work day without needing to be connected to the mains. Here's how to prolong that life-force and deal with a diminishing gas tank.

Above: Various things can take a toll on the battery life of your Mac, for example having too many apps open at one time.

Above: The F5 and F6 keys are used to control the keyboard backlight brightness.

Above: The F1 and F2 keys are used to adjust the brightness of the display.

Adjusting Screen/Keyboard Brightness

The brighter the screen, the more power it consumes. Use the F1 and F2 keys to change the display brightness and the F5 and F6 keys to adjust the keyboard backlight brightness. Every little helps.

Too Many Open Apps

You may not be working within them, but having all of those apps open in your dock takes up power, which takes up battery life. Just like we discussed in the Memory section, keeping only essential apps open helps your Mac's performance no-end.

Hot Tip

macOS features a neat tool within a drop-down battery meter in the menu bar, which informs you which apps are consuming 'significant battery life'. Shut these down or try alternatives.

Disable Connectivity

If you're not working online, or you're not using Bluetooth, turn them off. Having them constantly search for new networks or devices drinks battery life for fun.

Above: Use Energy Saver to set a certain amount of inactivity time as a prompt to put the display to sleep.

Update Your Apps And Software

Misfiring apps can have a negative affect on your battery life so ensure you're running the latest version by checking App Store > Updates. Generally speaking Apple's newest versions of macOS also come with under-the-hood improvements that allows a Mac to run efficiently. However, it's wise to do a quick Google search for any potential battery issues with that version before updating.

Give Your Mac A Nap

This is a security issue as well as a battery issue, but if you're stepping away from your screen for a few minutes, you should put your Mac to sleep. You can close the lid or select the Apple button from the menu bar and select Sleep. You can also use Energy Saver to configure periods of inactivity when the display or the system will go to sleep.

Above: Turn off the screen saver in order to lessen battery consumption.

Turn Off The Screen Saver

It's lovely to turn your Mac into a virtual photo slideshow when you're not using it, but that doesn't half take its toll on the battery. If you have a screen saver enabled, turn it off in System Preferences > Desktop and Screen Saver > Start After > Never.

Disconnect External Drives And Remote CD/DVDs

You know when you have a disc in your optical drive and you hear that whirring sound of the system checking the disc? That impacts your battery too.

No Battery Back-up(s)

Time Machine is great, but you don't necessarily want your Mac doing that hard work when you're on the train trying to finish some work and your battery life is down to 10 minutes. Within Time Machine, there's an option to disable back-ups while running your Mac on battery power.

WHAT IF BATTERY-SAVING STEPS DON'T WORK?

The steps outlined above should provide your battery with the ability to run longer without requiring a charge. However, there are still instances where these don't solve the issues of poor battery life. So what else could it possibly be?

Checking The Health Of Your Battery

There's a quick check you can make to ensure your battery is in good health. Head to About This Mac > More Information and then System Report. From there you can browse to Power > Battery Information > Condition. If it says 'Normal' it ain't the hardware at fault; if it says 'Replace Soon' you may want to head to the Apple Store and see about a replacement.

Above: Check whether a new battery is needed in System Report.

Thanks to the aluminium unibody design of most new MacBooks, replacing the battery yourself is not something that is recommended. Don't try. On much older MacBooks with a removable battery, you can do it yourself, just by unhooking the catch on the bottom of the device. You'll be able to find the correct replacement by checking the serial number on the existing battery.

Signs The Battery Is On The Way Out

There is only a finite number of charges you can give a MacBook battery before its performance begins trending downwards. Here are a few indicators that it's on the way out.

- **Can't hold a charge at all**: If you remove the power cable and your Mac switches off, you need a new battery.

- **Dramatic drop-offs**: If you're seeing a disproportionate fall in battery life at some stage in the cycle, you may need a new battery.

Above: The charger could be at fault if the battery is not charging.

CHARGING ISSUES

If your MacBook battery isn't holding a charge then it's almost certainly down to the battery itself. If it isn't charging at all, then that's a different matter entirely. The charger could be faulty or the charging port could be misfiring. If none of this applies to you or fixes your problem, chances are it is a battery failure.

Faulty Charger

If your MacBook is not charging, the first port of call is to try another charger. The bundled-in MacBook chargers can stand the odd bit of duress, but if you're constantly wrapping them up and taking them on the road, the cables will eventually give out. If a friend has a MacBook, then borrow their charger and give it a try. If that works, you'll need to get yourself a new one.

Software Issue

Sometimes, if a battery isn't charging it could be down to a software issue; your charger is plugged in, the computer recognizes that the charger is plugged in, but the battery is not charging. In these circumstances try the SMC reset explained on page 222. This may solve your problem.

Faulty Charging Port

In recent years Apple has switched from MagSafe magnetic charging connectors to the increasingly

Above: Charger cables may eventually give out.

popular USB-C port standard. While this gives the port more functionality, it's still more susceptible to damage, if you trip over your charging cable, for example. If you have a damaged charging port, it'll need repairing.

Left: Most Apple MacBooks now come with USB-C chargers.

KEYBOARD, MOUSE AND TRACKPAD ISSUES

We've come to take the humble keyboard, mouse and trackpad for granted, but if one or all of these bite the dust, your Mac is nigh on useless. Here's how to identify the problems.

IDENTIFYING AND SOLVING KEYBOARD PROBLEMS

There are few things more frustrating than your keyboard deserting you, whether it's USB, Bluetooth or built into your Mac. Here's how to identify the problems.

Keyboard, Mouse Or Trackpad Not Recognized

If your keyboard isn't functioning at all, it's more than likely to be a connectivity problem. Either the USB attachment is struggling or, in the case of wireless keyboards, Bluetooth is on the blink.

1. For wired keyboards and mice, check the USB connection or try a different port. Failing that, try the PRAM reset outlined on page 223.

2. For Bluetooth keyboards, your first port of call is to ensure the accessory is switched on at the side and the green light is on. Next check Bluetooth is switched on. If all that's in order try repairing the Mac as explained on page 168.

On/off
button

Above: When using an Apple Bluetooth keyboard a green light will inform you it is powered on.

3. On rare occasions Bluetooth signal interference can result in intermittent accessory performance. Try to ensure there are no metal objects between your peripheral and your Mac.

Accessory Battery Issues

Bluetooth-powered peripherals have their own batteries, but require very little power. They gain this power wirelessly through the Bluetooth connection. However, you can check the battery level of the device within the respective sections of System Preferences. If it's low, it'll need replacing. Here's some info on how – http://support.apple.com/kb/HT3050

The Keyboard Viewer

To test which keys are being recognized and which are not, you can head to Keyboard in System Preferences and select Show Keyboard & Character Viewer in the menu bar. You'll see it pop up

Above: The Keyboard & Character Viewer will help you identify which keys are being recognized and which are not.

Hot Tip

Before you go running to the
Apple Store, there's one time-tested
method you can try. Place the
MacBook and the keyboard in a
zip-lock bag filled with rice. It may
just do the trick; the rice sucking
out the moisture and returning
the keys to working order.

next to the battery monitor. Select
it. Now you can hit the keys and it'll
show which are being recognized and
which are not.

Moisture Problems

Have you spilt anything on your Mac?
Have you tried to clean the keyboard
with something a little too moist? Come
on, be honest now! Unresponsive keys
can often be caused by water damage.
It's not the end of the world, but it will
need fixing.

Using Dictation

If your keyboard isn't playing nicely and you absolutely have to get something down, you can
use the Mac's built-in dictation feature. This enables you to speak into the microphone and
then translates your speech into text. Head to System Preferences > Keyboard > Dictation and
turn on Dictation.

When within the text
field, tap the Function
key (fn) twice and
start speaking. When
you're finished, click
Done and the text will
appear on the screen.

Right: If Dictation is switched
on you can speak into the
microphone and the Mac
will convert it in to words.

I CAN'T GET ONLINE

Such is the modern dependence on the Internet that a lack of connectivity can undermine an entire day's work, ruin plans to enjoy a movie online, or cause social paralysis with the inability to check one's emails. Here are a few troubleshooting measures to help you rejoin the virtual world.

IS IT MY MAC?

Problems connecting to the Internet can be attributed to two things: the connection itself, or your Mac's inability to connect to it. More often than not it'll be the former. Firstly, check if other devices (smartphones, other computers) are able to connect to the network. If so, then it's time to take a look at your Mac's settings.

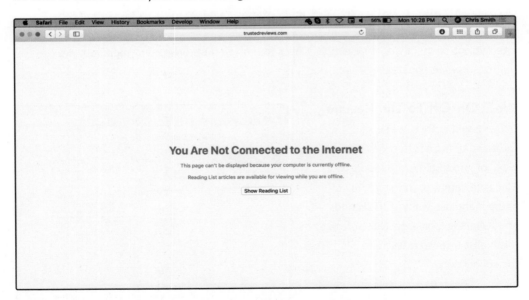

Above: If your Mac cannot connect to the Internet, check whether other devices have the same problem.

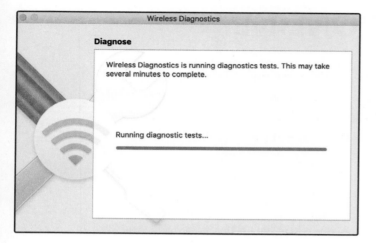

Network Preferences

If the signal indicator in the menu bar is full, your Mac has connected to the network but isn't pulling in Internet services. Hit the Option key and click the Wi-Fi icon in the menu bar. This will open a Wireless Diagnostics tool that can help you to resolve the issue.

Software Problems

Occasionally, when a new version of the software is released, it has a few bugs that need ironing out. Following the launch of macOS Mojave, some users complained about intermittent connectivity, for example. Check for known bugs online and keep your eye out for software updates.

Wi-Fi On/Off To The Rescue

If we've said it once, we've said it a thousand times; a restart can do the world of good. Before you restart your Mac completely, try turning Wi-Fi off in the menu bar, waiting 30 seconds and switching it back on. Quite often this is all it takes to resuscitate the connection.

Right: Try turning the Wi-Fi off briefly.

OUTAGES BEYOND YOUR CONTROL

If your Mac can't connect to the Internet then don't automatically blame your Mac. There could be other factors at play here.

Mo' Modem Mo' Problems

If you're struggling to connect, the first indicator that something might be wrong is the colour of the lights on your modem. If any of the indicators (Internet, Ethernet, Wireless, Power, etc.) change colour from the usual greens and blues to an amber or red (depending on your modem model) the connection isn't live. Immediately restart

the modem following the manufacturer's instructions. If that doesn't work, then it's likely there's a service outage. Call your provider or check for service updates online.

Check The Cable

It's always possible that your Ethernet cable could be faulty. If you're having problems with the wired connection, try to connect to Wi-Fi. If you're successful, it's probably a cable problem. If the same problem persists with a new/different cable, you may need to contact Apple for further support.

Above: If you can still connect to Wi-Fi, the Ethernet cable may be at fault.

EMAIL PROBLEMS

If you're connected to the Internet but not getting your email, or you can't configure your account, there are a few steps you can take to resolve issues with the Mail app.

Can't Configure Account

Apple plays nicely with the likes of Gmail, Yahoo and Hotmail – you know, the household names – but other accounts take a little extra configuration. If asked for account type (POP, IMAP, Exchange, etc.), incoming mail servers and outgoing servers you'll be able to find this information online, depending on your provider. If it's a work account, the easiest thing to do is to call on the IT guys to configure it for you.

Above: Some accounts are simple to set up; others may need more information.

Above: If an email won't send, try quitting the app and restarting.

Email Won't Send

Even when you're connected, Apple Mail has a frustrating habit of refusing to obey your commands to send mail. Sometimes you'll be greeted with a dialogue box that continually demands you enter your password, even though you've entered it correctly. Other times it will inform you the server is unavailable, and others it will sit in the outbox refusing to budge. In all cases you should try quitting the app and restarting, ensuring you save your draft first.

GENERAL MAC MAINTENANCE

Want to keep your Mac looking and acting as it did on the day you removed it from the box? There are a few steps you can take to preserve its prettiness.

CLEANING YOUR MAC

We know it's a bad habit, but when time is short, we often find ourselves eating and drinking while working, and pretty soon our Mac looks like the underside of a sofa cushion. Here are some tips for cleaning.

De-grossing Your Keyboard And Trackpad

Food for thought: the average keyboard contains more bacteria than a toilet seat. If that's not enough to encourage you to keep cleaner keys, then we're not sure what is. For external and internal peripherals, here are some tips.

1. Firstly, turn off your Mac or disconnect the keyboard if it is wired. If it is wireless, disconnect the battery.

2. Use a very slightly damp disinfectant wipe, which you can obtain from your local computing store.

3. Don't use regular kitchen wipes, household cleaners or bleach. They're too wet and could fry your logic board or kill the functionality of the device. Trust us, we speak from personal experience.

4. Using the wipe, lightly rub the trackpad, keys and the dividers until it appears clean.

5. Wipe with a slightly damp, smooth cloth.

6. Dry the keyboard off with a dry, smooth cloth. Don't use tissue or rough cloths or towels.

7. Failure to do this correctly could fry your keyboard leading, in the case of MacBooks, to an expensive repair bill.

Cleaning The Screen

Macs aren't touch screen, but that doesn't mean they don't get pawed by children or sneezed on from time to time. If you've splashed out extra coin on a Retina Display MacBook, then you'll want to keep those extra pixels looking pristine.

1. Turn off your Mac or disconnect the display.

2. Use a dry, smooth, lint-free cloth to wipe away the dust.

3. Use a damp, smooth, lint-free cloth to clean the display, avoiding openings.

4. Dry with another dry, smooth cloth.

Above: Follow these steps to keep your Mac screen clean, especially if it's a Retina Display MacBook.

5. You can also purchase screen wipes from pretty much every electronics store in the world. Invest in these and make sure they don't contain alcohol or aren't overly damp.

ImPORTant Cleaning Information

How about those all important charging, USB and Thunderbolt ports? They can get very dusty and that dust can sometimes harm your Mac's ability to connect to them. Under no circumstances should you use damp cloths to attempt to clean these. It'll fry the inside. Lightly wipe with a smooth dry cloth to remove dust.

MORE HELP IS AT HAND

We've done our best to assist with the most common complaints Mac users suffer, but frankly we'd need a whole volume of books to go through them all. There's plenty of additional help online, while you can also call on Apple to fix your issue.

APPLE ONLINE SUPPORT

While we'd love to make ourselves available to answer all of your questions and solve all of your problems, if you're suffering from one of the rarer problems not mentioned here, you can seek help from Apple's online FAQs or the vast community of helpful Apple enthusiasts who could provide the solution to your problems.

Above: Apple provides online support to help answer your questions and solve any problems.

Above: Select your Mac product for specific advice.

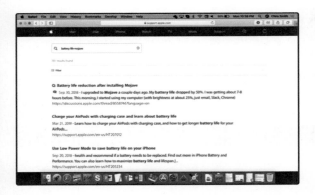

Above: Search the forums for help from others with similar issues.

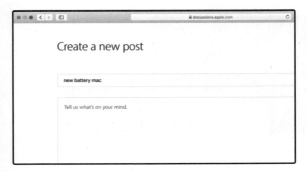

Above: If you can't find the answer, post a message on the forum.

Apple's Support Website

Before you call tech support or book an appointment at your local Apple Store, you can check online for common issues and instructions on how to use your Mac's features. Head to apple.com/support/mac, find your product, find your issue and make use of the information.

Searching The Forums

The Apple community forums are awash with users who are enduring problems with their Macs. Type discussions.apple.com into your web browser and input your problem into the Search Communities box. Chances are someone else has had your issue and it has been solved.

Posting On The Discussion Forums

If you can't find a solution to your problem, then you can post a question of your own. Fellow Mac users are happy to attempt

Hot Tip

Be sure only to act upon advice within your comfort level. We'd advise against doing anything in 'Terminal' if you're not experienced in this area.

answers as helpful responses earn them reputation points. From the Discussions site, browse to your device's specific forum or to the macOS forums and submit your question. You'll need to log in with your Apple ID. Helpfully, you can choose to receive an alert when a user responds to your post.

TIME TO CALL IN THE GENIUSES

If there's a hardware or software issue that's beyond your skillset, you can go straight to Apple.

AppleCare

AppleCare is Apple's extended warranty service. When you buy a Mac it comes with a one-year warranty. After that you need AppleCare to cover you for tech support, software help, hardware failure and accidental damage. You can call on telephone or in-store support. It covers you for up to three years after you buy your Mac. We know it's really tough to stomach finding an extra £100–200 on top of the expensive Mac you've already bought, but you run the risk of paying out a whole lot more if you don't. Can you afford to be without it? If your battery dies? You'll get a replacement. If your charger is faulty? You'll get a replacement. If the hard drive fails? You get the idea.

AppleCare
Protection Plan

Hot Tip

If you buy AppleCare at the time of purchase, you'll be automatically registered with your proof of purchase. If you're buying after the fact, you can register here – http://www. apple.com/retail/geniusbar/.

Telephone Support

When you buy your Mac, you get 90 days of free, unlimited telephone support. If you have the AppleCare extended warranty, you'll get access to extensive technical and how-to support for up to three years. Usually, they'll aim to solve your problem in a phone call.

In-store Support

One of the few pitfalls of owning a Mac is that only Apple and its authorized service providers can/should fix them.

If you're having a problem with your Mac, you can head into your nearest Apple Store (they're in most big cities now) and seek help, book a repair, or get a replacement. It's best to book an appointment at a Genius Bar (Apple's pretentious name for its in-store experts) online at http://www.apple.com/uk/retail/geniusbar/ or you can go into the store and make an appointment. If you require a repair, your issue warranty status will determine whether you have to pay for it or not.

If Your Mac Needs A Repair

If your Mac needs attention and you take it to the store, you can part with it there and then. Mostly, they'll fix it within a week. You can pick it up or have it delivered. If you call tech support and a repair is arranged, you can take it to an Apple Store or authorized service provider, or you can have a technician visit, provided you have AppleCare.

One-to-one Support

We'd hope that by buying this book, you won't need this, but if you've bought your Mac from Apple in the last 90 days, you're entitled to a Personal Setup session at your local Apple Store where they'll help you with set-up and any usage questions you might have.

Your Rights

Apple's website points out there are differences between its own warranty and consumer law. It's website says: 'For consumers who are covered by consumer protection laws or regulations in their country of purchase or, if different, their country of residence, the benefits conferred by Apple's One Year Limited Warranty are in addition to all rights and remedies conveyed by such consumer protection laws and regulations, including but not limited to the rights described below.' If you think your consumer rights stretch beyond what Apple is offering you, be sure to point that out.

Hot Tip

Head to http://concierge.apple.com/reservation/gb/en/workshop/ to find out about free Mac workshops at your local Apple Store.

100 TOP APPS

Throughout this book we've focused on the built-in Mac apps, but there's a whole world of third-party software out there just waiting to enhance your computing experience. Here's our top 100 available either online or from the Mac App Store.

GAMES
1. Stardew Valley
2. Civilization VI
3. Minecraft
4. World of Warcraft: Battle for Azeroth
5. Night In The Woods
6. Fortnite: Battle Royale
7. Rocket League
8. Kerbal Space Program
9. Donut County
10. Life Is Strange
11. Lego Star Wars

SOCIAL MEDIA AND COMMUNICATION
1. Tweetbot
2. Skype
3. WhatsApp Desktop
4. Spark

5. Self-Control
6. Mail for Gmail
7. Thunderbird
8. Tweetdeck
9. Buffer
10. Pin Pro
11. Trillian
12. Slack

INTERNET
1. Google Chrome
2. Firefox
3. Opera
4. Onmiweb
5. 1Password
6. Deliveries
7. Reeder 3
8. Hotspot Shield VPN
9. Transmit 5
10. Google Earth For Mac
11. AdBlock Plus for Safari

BACK-UP AND ONLINE STORAGE

1. Google Drive
2. Dropbox
3. Mega
4. Microsoft OneDrive
5. Backblaze
6. Backup Scheduler

SECURITY AND UTILITIES

1. Duet
2. Microsoft Remote Desktop
3. Dr Cleaner
4. Unclutter
5. Bartender
6. DropZone 3
7. Transmission
8. Handbrake
9. Little Snitch
10. The Unarchiver
11. Alfred
12. OnmiDiskSweeper
13. Duplicate Detective
14. Moom
15. Tooth Fairy
16. Trash Me

PRODUCTIVITY

1. Microsoft Office
2. Copied
3. Agenda
4. Evernote
5. ReadKit
6. Magnet
7. Wunderlist
8. Todoist
9. iBooks Author
10. Voice Memos
11. Day One
12. iA Writer
13. Grammar Checker
14. Amphetamine
15. Franz
16. Fantastical
17. Bear Notes
18. Wave Box

CREATIVE TOOLS

1. Adobe Photoshop
2. Final Cut Pro
3. Adobe Premiere Elements
4. Polarr
5. Touch Retouch
6. Logic Pro
7. Autodeck Sketchbook
8. GIMP

9. Pixelmator
10. Affinity Photos
11. GIF Brewery

ENTERTAINMENT

1. Spotify
2. VLC
3. Vimeo
4. GIPHY Capture
5. Kindle
6. Stream To Chromecast
7. Audacity
8. Garageband
9. Capo 3
10. Boom 2
11. Vox
12. Djay Pro 2
13. Delicious Library
14. myTuner

INDEX